Heaven
Your Real Home

Joni Eareckson Tada

ADULT EDITION

LifeWay Press
Nashville, Tennessee

Heaven Your Real Home

Dewey Decimal Classification: 236.24
Subject Heading: HEAVEN

This book is the text for course CG-0223 in the subject area Personal Life in the
Christian Growth Study Plan.

Unless otherwise indicated, Scripture quotations are from the Holy Bible, New
International Version, copyright ©1973, 1978, 1984 by International Bible Society.
Other versions used: King James Version, (KJV).

Printed in the United States of America

LifeWay Press
127 Ninth Avenue, North
Nashville, Tennessee 37234-0151

Contents

Authors

Joni Eareckson Tada is founder and president of JAF Ministries (Joni and Friends), an organization that reaches out to the disabled community with Christian witness and encouragement. Her first book *Joni,* which tells the story of the diving accident that left her a quadriplegic at age 17, has been translated in over 40 languages. Living in a wheelchair since 1967 has taught Joni about faith and suffering and has given her a longing for her heavenly home. Meanwhile, she has learned how to paint by holding a pencil or brush in her teeth and is a sought-after artist; recording artist; and television, video, and radio personality. She conducts workshops nationwide and travels around the world assisting persons with disabilities and their families. Joni was appointed to the National Council on Disability under Presidents Reagan and Bush. She and her husband Ken have been married for more than 13 years and live in Calabasas, California.

Dale W. McCleskey wrote the interactive learning activities and group leader guide. Dale is editor of LIFE Support Group Series materials and other undated products for the Discipleship and Family Adult Department at the Baptist Sunday School Board. He pastored for 15 years and has written or co-authored 12 books. Dale and his wife Cheryl have two children. Dale has a passion for ministry to hurting people. He currently serves as support group minister and deacon at Gladeville Baptist Church in Nashville, Tennessee.

Introduction

I'm an artist. I have to confess, though, I've never succeeded in painting a picture of heaven. People have asked me why, and I haven't come up with a good answer, except to say that heaven defies the blank canvas of the artist. The best I can offer are scenes of breathtaking mountains or clouds that halfway reflect something of heaven's majesty. I'm never quite able to achieve the effect.

And neither is earth. Actual mountains and clouds are exalting, but even the most beautiful displays of earth's glory—towering thunderheads above a wheat field or the view of the Grand Canyon from the south rim—are only rough sketches of heaven. Earth's best is only a dim reflection of the glory that will one day be revealed.

Trouble is, we rarely let that fact sink in. That is, until we are stopped short by one of those brilliant nights when the air is clear like crystal and the black sky studded with a million stars. It takes such a moment to make us pause and think, "What is your life? You are a mist that appears for a little while and then vanishes" (James 4:14).

Then we rush indoors to catch the six o'clock news or referee an argument between our kids. The heavenly moment is lost and we think, *Life doesn't seem like a mist that quickly vanishes.*

We really don't believe it's all going to end, do we? If God hadn't told us differently, we'd think this parade of life would go on forever.

But it will end. This life is not forever, nor is it the best life that will ever be. The fact is that believers are headed for heaven. It is reality. What we do here on earth has a direct bearing on how we will live there. Heaven may be as near as next year, or next week; so it makes good sense to spend some time here on earth thinking candid thoughts about that marvelous future reserved for us.

How This Study Works

Welcome to *Heaven...Your Real Home.* In this group study edition you will do more than simply read a book. I want you to be involved, to work with the Scriptures, and to journey with me through what we know about heaven. I have provided you with some activities to help you make this journey. You will find different assignments. Some will look like the following.

 Have you experienced a moment when you saw or heard an echo of heaven? If so, think about that moment of wonder or beauty. Take a moment and ask God to speak to you in this study.

When you see the 🕊 symbol I will ask you to do a non-writing assignment such as praying about what you have been reading. At other times you will see a symbol that looks like this ✍. I will ask you to make a written response. Studies demonstrate that people learn more when they complete the learning activities. Please don't skip over the learning activities and deprive yourself of an opportunity to grow. You will also need to complete the activities so you can participate fully in your study group.

How I Came to This Study

Years ago when I became paralyzed in a diving accident, my world was reduced to the basics. Lying for two years in a hospital bed on starched sheets surrounded by starched hospital workers, I lived in a sterile vacuum, doing little more than eating, breathing, and sleeping. I had all the time in the world to ask questions of God.

Perhaps friends who visited me thought I was being too philosophical. But they weren't faced with the larger-than-life questions that were plaguing me: What is the meaning to life? Where are we all heading? Haunted and hurting, I realized life had to be more than just existing.

That's when I came face-to-face with the God of the Bible. I decided it was better to throw my questions at Him rather than shrug my shoulders and turn away. Those two years in the hospital were like one long question-and-answer session.

Heaven...Your Real Home is, in part, a result of that time of questioning. What is the meaning to life? To know and glorify God. Where are we all heading? To enjoy Him forever—at least for those who know Him.

It's odd to express appreciation to a wheelchair, but I do. Almost 30 years of quadriplegia, and almost as many studying God's Word, have deepened my gratitude to God for these bolts and bars. The chair has shown me the way home by heart.

I thank you for taking the time to join me on this journey toward heavenly glories above. And who knows. Perhaps before you finish reading, you'll discover you know the way home by heart too.

What You'll Learn from This Study

I have designed the following pages to point the way: guides and signposts to point you to heaven, the real home of our hearts and spirit. I want to tap on your heart, open up a map, and show you the way home. The thoughts contained here are for those whose hearts break for heavenly joy, or at least would like to have their hearts break for heaven. It's even for those who don't have the faintest idea about heavenly joy but are haunted with curiosity.

As you poise your pencil to begin each lesson, remember the most important part: Begin in prayer. Prayer is the language of heaven; it is the code through which you will be able to decipher heaven's hieroglyphics. God will reveal so much more to you when you first ask Him to do so in prayer.

This book was not written as a theology text. My purpose was not to present a doctrinal argument. Christians have many views of end-times events. Don't get caught up in whether or not you agree with my views. If you do, you will miss the purpose of this study.

The purpose is to increase your passion for heaven. I want you to compare your attitude at the end of the study with your attitude at the beginning. I pray that you will grow in your knowledge of what the Bible says about heaven, in your desire—even homesickness—for heaven, and in your zeal to see others as citizens of heaven. Most of all I hope that you will grow in your fervent love for the Lord Jesus, for where He is, there is heaven.

Using This Resource in a Group Setting
You will benefit much more from this study if you participate in a group. The group leader guide begins on page 155. I urge you to do the lessons each day and then to meet with a group of believers to process your work in the unit.

Let's Get Started
True, heaven may defy the printed page of the author, but words and pictures can sometimes strike a resonant chord, helping us hear that ancient and heavenly song which the morning stars sang together. Rather than let that song retire in the presence of mundane things like scratchy AM radios and grinding dishwashers, I hope the following pages will help you tune into heaven's melody.

Like stealing a tiny sip of stew before dinner, it's meant to be a foretaste of what to expect when you get to the banquet table.

It's meant to point you to the sky and help you see something far, far beyond the constellation of Ursa Major.

Let's not get too settled in, too satisfied with the good things down here on earth. They are only the tinkling sounds of the orchestra warming up. The real song is about to break into a heavenly symphony, and its prelude is only a few moments away.

> Joni Eareckson Tada
> JAF Ministries
> P.O. Box 3333
> Agoura Hills, California 91301

Unit 1

What's So Great About Heaven?

*L*et your imagination run wild for a moment. Jesus has gone on to prepare a place for us, and each of us is to have a big mansion—no down payment or mortgage to worry about, thankfully—on a golden avenue overlooking acres of fields and flowers. Wow!

Or for you, not "wow."

Perhaps, "Well, . . . that's nice."

When it comes to a glass house on a golden street, you may be tempted to throw a stone through the glass, out of sheer gumption, to see if celestial plate glass cracks. Or maybe you're simply feeling awkward and uncomfortable in God's glittering, golden throne room. For that matter, you're still hung up in this tangle of earthly imagery whenever you picture heaven. You see yourself seated at the wedding feast of the Lamb where, presumably, there's no need for air-conditioning or central heating in the banquet hall. But where do you draw the line in dispensing with the paraphernalia of earth when picturing heaven? If the banquet is to be eaten decently, surely we will need knives and forks and pots and pans to cook stuff in. Mixers must be somewhere in the background, and who does the dishes? People in hell?[1]

I can understand if these images don't make you yearn for your heavenly dwelling. It's not that you're absorbed by the things of earth; it's just that heaven doesn't feel like home. Yet the images painted in the Bible represent something designed to grip your heart, possess your soul, and call forth a powerful homesickness that makes you want to hurry up and unlock the front door of that mansion of yours.

Wouldn't it be nice to feel nostalgic for heaven that way?

What You'll Learn in This Unit

In this unit you will explore basic questions about heaven. Why do some aspects of heaven seem less than appealing? How can we develop positive images of heaven? Where is heaven, and how do we get there?

Unit Scripture

Then I saw a new heaven and a new earth, for the first heaven and the first earth had passed away, and there was no longer any sea. —Revelation 21:1

Jeremiah 11.6 b 5

Lesson 1
Why Do Heaven's Symbols Sound So Negative?

I love thinking and reading about heaven. I've noticed as I've flipped through the pages of Scripture—our best resource about heaven—that its language is cryptic. You almost have to crack heaven's hieroglyphics before any of it makes sense.

What's more, I've gotten lost in the chronological chaos, wondering how Jesus' return to earth connects with the millennium, the rapture, the judgment, the bowls, scrolls, and trumpets in the Book of Revelation. How can we pursue heaven through so much confusion if we keep stumbling over word pictures of crowns and thrones?

These images only seem to be deterrents. They actually are incentives. The symbols of palms, crowns, streets of gold, and seas of glass used in Scripture are just that—symbols.

 Think of a symbol you encounter regularly—it could be anything from a comma in a sentence to a stop sign. How closely does the symbol represent what it symbolizes? Below describe the purpose of a symbol.

_____

One purpose of a symbol is to represent in a simple way a more complex action or idea. Symbols never quite satisfy our curiosity about heaven, and they're not meant to. They are only shadowy images of the real thing, as well as guides and signposts that show us the way home.

One such signpost in my life occurred a few years after the 1967 diving accident in which I became paralyzed. I was just beginning to get my spiritual act together with Jesus, having been pressed up against a wall that caused me to seriously consider His lordship in my life. I spent long evenings with my friend Steve Estes as he pored over his open Bible.

He was guiding me through the Word of God to help me learn about heaven. Immediately, he had my attention. Everybody wants to go to heaven. We are all curious to know where it is, how it looks, who's there, and what they wear and do. I'm no exception.

Symbols are incentives.

One day you will have a new glorified body.

I was fascinated to discover that one day I would no longer be paralyzed but have a new glorified body. Immediately I began imagining all the wonderful things I would do with resurrected hands and legs: swim a couple of laps, peel a few oranges, sprint across fields and splash into waves, scale a few rocks and skip through meadows. Such thoughts enraptured me. Sitting there in a wheelchair and unable to move, I began to sense a longing, a rising echo of that heavenly song about to stretch wide open my heart's capacity for joy.

Sensing my wonder with it all, Steve pointed me to a passage in Revelation 21. I couldn't wait to read all about this future God was reserving for us. I picked it up with the first verse:

"'Then I saw a new heaven and a new earth for the first heaven and the first earth had passed away . . .'"

"Wait a minute, you mean everything about this earth will disappear and pass away? But there are lots of things I like. Chili dogs with cheese. The NBA playoffs. Bridal Veil Falls at Yosemite National Park."

"'. . . and there was no longer any sea.'"

"What! No sea? But I love the ocean. The waves. The wind. The smell of salt in the air. What about splashing in the breakers? What about digging my toes in the sand? To me, heaven has to have oceans in it."

"'I saw the Holy City, the new Jerusalem, coming down out of heaven from God, prepared as a bride beautifully dressed for her husband.'"

"No seas? No sand dunes? No Great Barrier Reef? No fields of wheat or sequoia trees? That does it! I hate cities, even if they are holy. Who wants 16-story housing projects in the center of heaven? Some people may like perfect urban planning, but not me, brother."

 Time out! Have you feared the loss of certain things when you get to heaven? ❑ Yes ❑ No

If so, in the margin list at least three things you fear you might miss.

My friend closed his Bible. He sensed my disappointment. He knew that as quickly as the wonder of heaven had risen in my heart, it had disappeared. Something was terribly wrong, either with me or with the Bible's descriptions of heaven.

Sound familiar?

Heaven Defies Description

Be honest. Be like any red-blooded, right-thinking Christian with both feet planted firmly on earth. Haven't there been times when word pictures of heaven from the Bible fall flat and boring next to the breathtaking sight and thunderous roar of Niagara Falls? Or scanning the serene Colorado plains from the pinnacle of Pikes Peak? Or swaying with the motion of acres of rippling waves of golden grain? Do you sense that sometimes the musical notes of God's creation almost eclipse Ezekiel's footnotes describing things in heaven as wheels that intersect other wheels as well as move in four directions? "Their rims were high and awesome, and all four rims were full of eyes all around" (Ezekiel 1:18). Whhaat?

"This is upsetting. I don't understand," I said to Steve.

Do you sometimes feel less than excited thinking about heaven? ❑ Yes ❑ No From the following list of common ideas about heaven, check each one that does not make you want to get on the next bus. Add your own.

❑ sitting on a cloud, strumming a harp
❑ sitting in a worship service
❑ golden streets
❑ a mansion
❑ being perfect
❑ other _____

To encourage me, Steve flipped to Jesus' words in John 14:1–4, " 'Do not let your hearts be troubled. Trust in God; trust also in me. In my Father's house are many rooms; if it were not so, I would have told you. I am going there to prepare a place for you. And if I go and prepare a place for you, I will come back and take you to be with me that you also may be where I am. You know the way to the place where I am going.'"

My friend tried to excite my imagination, explaining that if Jesus is presently preparing heaven, it must be out-of-sight. He only required seven days to create the earth; He's had almost two thousand years to work on my room in His mansion.

Steve sighed. "Joni, you know the Bible well enough to realize it won't steer you wrong. So rather than put us off, shouldn't such descriptions ignite our hearts? Aren't you just a little relieved that heaven can't be reduced to terms we can manage?"

Jesus is preparing a place for you.

I looked at him blankly.

"Doesn't it console you to think that its marvels defy description?" He paused a long minute, then added, "Simply put, there are no words for heaven." Now it was his turn to look at me blankly.

"But your longings about heaven have to hang on something," my friend warned. "You can't ignore streets of gold and rainbow thrones just because they don't thrill you at first glance. They're the images God gave us—the symbols Scripture invites us to ponder. They're not deterrents to your faith, they're incentives."

 Would you be willing to pray, asking God to give you the wisdom to understand these biblical glimpses of heaven? He promises that He answers such prayers and He never shames you for not already knowing (see James 1:5 in the margin). Careful now, asking God for wisdom is no shortcut to avoid Bible study, but it is a great place to begin.

If any of you lacks wisdom, he should ask God, who gives generously to all without finding fault, and it will be given to him.
–James 1:5

I knew my friend Steve was right on this point too. If I skirted the glittering celestial city with jasper walls 200 feet thick — just because I didn't like the idea of urban planning in heaven—I'd have nothing to hang my faith on but my imagination. And that could be dangerous, if not a little New Age-ish.

Slowly the light dawned. The problem lay not with the Bible's descriptions of heavenly glories, but with the way I was looking at those symbols.

I didn't realize it at the time, but Steve Estes had just shown me how to read the map, how to understand the legend and symbols that would show me the way home to heaven. When it comes to heaven, there is no limit to what the Lord will confide to those whose faith is rooted in Scripture.

 You have begun to share my journey—the journey to explore and learn about heaven. Describe one positive attitude about heaven you already have.

_____

 Identify one negative attitude or question about heaven you would like to examine.

_____

Lesson 2

Why Is Heaven Difficult to Understand?

*R*eading about heaven in Scripture can almost sound like bad copy in a tour book:

> *A large set of pearl-studded gates will welcome you to heaven, but be careful of slippery roads paved with gold. Don't bother looking for interesting local cuisine as there is no need to eat while in heaven, neither will you need to look for lodging since comfortable beds, crisp sheets, and downy pillows have no purpose.*
>
> *Topping the list of scenic points is a sea of glass. Do not miss the spectacular New Jerusalem, a striking city of the future, employing award-winning architectural design. Marvel at its 12 foundations. Stand amazed before its 12 gates, each made of a gigantic, single pearl. For sheer spectacle, the New Jerusalem eclipses even the Emerald City of Oz.*

As weird and strange as the word pictures are, they convey one thing for certain: The whole scene in heaven is very real. There's nothing wispy or vaporous about the exact measurements of a 12-layered foundation of precious stones. It's real, but entirely alien to anything people have heard of on earth.

God has good reasons for describing heaven this way. If we were able to break down the infinitely high wall that separates "everything that is spiritual" from "everything that is not spiritual," if we could scale that wall with human understanding, then our faith wouldn't mean very much.

 Here's a self-examination question. When it comes to heaven, have you tended to accept your own ideas or what you've heard, or have you carefully based your thinking on a study of Scripture? Place a mark on the scale below.

Depended on my ideas　　　　　　　　　*Searched the Scriptures*

Heaven is very real.

Heaven Is a Mystery

God designed both heaven and humans so that a cloud of mystery would prevent you and me from fully grasping heaven with language and logic. The apostle Paul, like Ezekiel and John, saw heaven; unlike them, he was not permitted to describe the sights! The mystery remains intact. We cannot fashion heaven solely out of the Lincoln Logs of our logic. Even if we could, we would merely be illuminating the sun with a flashlight. We only break through the glass darkly by faith.

My friend Steve Estes used this analogy. "Joni, don't mistake signs in the Bible for the reality they only represent. It's like this: Suppose we're driving down the road and see a green highway sign that reads, 'Chicago: 50 miles.' In no way would we mistake that road sign for Chicago, right?"

"Right."

"We both understand it's pointing us down the road to a reality far beyond a 5x8-foot green sign with white lettering."

This was easy to track.

"In the same way, don't walk up to a wall 1,400 miles high made of sparkling jewels and stop there. Don't get down on all fours to examine whether the gold streets are 18-karat as opposed to 24-karat. These things are only pointing to a mind-boggling reality far beyond mere symbols."

Steve charged ahead. "Since you seem less than enthusiastic about the New Jerusalem, consider this: Its walls are said to be the same height, width, and length. The city is a perfect cube of 1,400 mile proportions. What do you think that means?"

"That heaven's ugly," I replied.

"Watch it or you'll smack your face on a Chicago road sign," he laughed. "If you stop with only the symbol, it's not a pretty sight. But symbols point away from themselves to something else."

We turned to the Old Testament description of King Solomon constructing the holy of holies in the ancient temple in Jerusalem, the room where the ark of the covenant rested.

"You see," he said, "the proportions are identical, only heaven is said to be about a quarter of a million times larger. Since the Book of Revelation insists that no temple is found in heaven, the idea is probably that paradise is all temple. Just as God's dazzling presence filled the holy of holies, so it will fill that holy city, only more intensely."

"Hmmm . . . that's something to think about," I mused.

"Exactly! You have to think. When you take time to ponder Scripture, your faith has something to hold onto, something that's factual and true. Your faith has something to feed on, something from which your dreams about heaven can take root."

 Have you smacked your head on any Chicago road signs? Make a list of images about heaven you have held that you might just be mistaken about. Write them in the margin and be prepared to share your list with your group.

Sunshine to My Heart

What he was saying was darkness to my intellect but sunshine to my heart. He was right. I wanted those streets of gold and pearly gates to ignite my heart, not throw ice water on it. My heart wanted heaven to be the tuning fork God strikes. I wanted the deepest part of me to vibrate with that ancient yet familiar longing, that desire for something that would fill and overflow my soul.

I smiled. Then we both smiled. We knew God had not brought us this far only to disappoint me with mere negatives. I was not about to be daunted. There must be positives.

 You're doing this study, so you probably want your heart to thrill to the thought of heaven, too. Read in Mark 9:24 what the father of a young sick child said about his faith. The verse is printed in the margin. Take time to pray. Tell God about your heaven excitement. Ask Him to help your "un-excitement."

Immediately the boy's father exclaimed, "I do believe; help me overcome my unbelief!" –Mark 9:24

The Bible is a book to be trusted, so there must be more behind the rainbow throne than met the eye. All this stuff about golden cities and seas of glass had to be clues in some amazing mystery. And if Psalm 25:14 was correct, if "the Lord confides in those who fear him," then it's a mystery that God intends to stimulate me to seek until I grasp what heaven is about.

I'm thankful heaven is grander than human language. Trying to grasp heaven without faith is like trying to admire the outside of a huge great cathedral with grand windows. Standing outside, you see an impressive but imposing structure. The building is striking, but has no real glory. But if you go inside the cathedral, you are breathless as you stand washed in glorious colors from the light that streams through the windows.[2] This image is a little like looking at heaven through eyes of faith.

But our citizenship is in heaven. And we eagerly await a Savior from there, the Lord Jesus Christ.
–Philippians 3:20

How would you answer the critic who says, "Why bother to think about heaven now?"

_____

_____

_____

_____

Faith takes us beyond the imposing and impressive language of golden cities and thrones and reveals the better, brighter glory inside the walls of the New Jerusalem. Faith takes the descriptions of 24-karat asphalt and big pearls swinging on hinges and makes us certain that what we hope for is far, far better than here.

The Bible provides the symbols. But faith makes the hieroglyphics of heaven come alive. And heaven has to come alive! You're a citizen of the kingdom of heaven and according to Philippians 3:20, you're supposed to be eagerly awaiting it. Heaven is your journey's end, your life's goal, your purpose for going on. If heaven is the home of your spirit, the rest for your soul, the repository of every spiritual investment on earth, then it must grip your heart. Your heart must grip heaven by faith.

 Complete the activity in the margin.

 Review this lesson. Circle one statement, Scripture, or idea that heightens your eagerness for heaven. Ask God to increase your passion for Him.

Lesson 3

How Can I Turn the "Negatives" into Positives?

I'm struck that heaven is often described in terms of "no this" and "no that." No more sea. No more night. No more time. No more moon or sun. What about food, marriage, art, and great books? Do the other benefits in heaven outweigh the "no this" and "no that"? Sitting in a wheelchair for decades has loaded me with a lifetime of glorious memories, everything from feeling my fingers on the cool ivory keys of a piano to the euphoria of diving through the breakers at high tide. Such memories flood my being and thus, my imagination. It's awful to think that the best stuff of which memories are made will have no place in heaven. You could say the same.

"However," Steve challenged, "'as it is written: No eye has seen, no ear has heard, no mind has conceived what God has prepared for those who love him' (1 Corinthians 2:9). Your imagination can't begin to picture all that God has in store."

"Well then," I fumed, "God can't expect us to get very excited about heaven. If I've got to stomp underfoot all the wonderful things I enjoy about earth just so heaven can come off looking better, then count me out."

It was lost on me how so much of heaven's happiness could be described in negative terms. Why did God seem to talk about heaven in terms of what it will not be, rather than what it will be?

That's not all. I was also struck that the positive descriptions about heaven seem clumsy and ungraceful. Rainbow thrones? Streets of gold? Pearly gates? A glittering city 1,400 miles in length and as wide and high as it is long with walls 200 feet thick and made of jasper? It more closely resembled Minnesota's monolithic Mall of America. I was embarrassed to admit it, but even the descriptions about everlasting peace and eternal felicity seemed boring.

No food, no marriage, no moon, no need for good books?

Faith reminds us that every negative is only the reverse side of a fulfilling of all that God intended our humanity to be. True, we may enjoy a good charcoal-broiled steak or a night of romance with our spouse under a full moon, but faith tells us these things are inklings of better tastes and enraptured delights yet to come. They won't be negated; rather, the whisper of what they are on earth will find complete fulfillment in heaven.

 Review your life. Remember things that were terribly important to you at an earlier stage of your life—like playing with dolls or trucks when you were five. In the margin list one such item or activity for each life stage you have experienced.

You probably don't get excited about riding a tricycle today, yet when you were age three such play was ecstacy. If you told a three-year-old you were taking away her trike so she could drive a car, she would probably be terrified.

Use your eyes of faith. Think of the "no more's" in terms of "future divine fulfillments." See that every negative is just a reverse side of a fulfilling. What is no longer needed for biological purposes, such as procreation or digestion, may serve a far higher, more beautiful function.

This thought is one of those realities that goes beyond sense or sight. Consider the words, "Blessed is the man that endureth

Your imagination can't begin to picture all that God has in store.

childhood _____

_____

preteen _____

_____

teenage _____

_____

young adult _____

_____

median adult _____

_____

temptation: for when he is tried, he shall receive the crown of life" (James 1:12, KJV). From a verse like this we can infer that when we curb our appetites on earth and refuse to let lust and gluttony ruin wonderful things like marriage or food, our victories gain glory and splendor in heaven. If we controlled our hormones on earth, then fidelity in marriage will serve us in eternity as a triumphant weapon with which we defeated temptation. All this will bring greater glory to God.

I broached this subject of "controlling hormones" on another one of those pleasant evenings around the fireplace with Steve. It was the big question everybody wonders about heaven sooner or later. I casually remarked, "What's this stuff about 'no marriage in heaven' supposed to mean?"

He seemed to read my mind, and smiling, he said, "Joni, things like procreation and digestion are physical functions necessary for our life here on earth. Heaven promises something far, far better. Far better than even the pleasure people enjoy in marriage."

I looked at him with skepticism. "I'm not married, but that's pretty hard to imagine."

"No, it's not hard to imagine, it's impossible. Absolutely impossible. We have no idea what God is preparing. But look at this verse in Psalm 16:11," he said as he flipped back to the Old Testament. "'You will fill me with joy in your presence, with eternal pleasures at your right hand.' Faith tells us that the pleasures and the privileges people enjoy in marriage are only hints and whispers of greater delights yet to come."

I gave him a doubtful grin. I decided he was right. My questions about intimacy and food would have to be shoved to the back burner for the time being. I would have to cultivate faith that every negative is only the reverse side of a fulfilling, a fulfilling of all that God intended our humanity to be.

Every negative is only the reverse side of a fulfilling.

We will not lose in heaven. We will gain. The Lord who has planted the seed of future divine fulfillments in almost every good thing on earth will carry it on to completion until the day He arrives and makes crystal clear all the unseen divine realities. God won't throw any good thing away.

See into the Positives

May I pose a question that will explain something else about all those negatives in heaven? Do you know why a photographer uses a negative to take your photo? He uses it to show us a positive image. I use the same principle when I paint at my easel. Sometimes I choose not to outline a shape, such as a leaf, with a brush, but rather I paint the sky all around the leaf, which then defines its shape. It's called "negative space" painting, and it's a way — some would say a better way — of giving definition to the shapes of leaves against a sky. The artist helps you see by painting what you don't see.

The principle is the same when it comes to heaven: The negatives are used in order to show us the positive. On earth, we know all too well what the negatives are: suffering, pain, and death. Show us their opposites, the positive side, and we shall have the best possible idea of the perfect state. For instance, there may be no moon, no marriage, and no need to eat in heaven, as suggested in Revelation 21, but there are also some pretty good negatives we can relate to in Revelation 21 also.

No more sorrow.

No more crying.

No more pain.

No more curse.

And, praise God, no more death.

Selah. Pause. Think of that.

We'd all admit that the sum of human misery on earth vastly outweighs the sum of human happiness. Job said, "Man born of woman is of few days and full of trouble" (14:1). David the psalmist expresses this in Psalm 55:6, 8: "Oh, that I had the wings of a dove! I would fly away and be at rest. I would hurry to my place of shelter, far from the tempest and storm."

I'm with Job and David: Get me outta here!

 Have you ever felt that way? In the margin write a brief description of the time in your life that you came closest to saying get me outta here!

I can't tell you how much sorrow I've held at bay over the years. Tears could come easily if I allowed myself to think of all the pleasures of movement and sensation I've missed. Diving into a pool and feeling my arms and legs slice through the water. Plucking guitar strings with my fingers. Jogging till my muscles burn. Cracking steam-broiled Maryland crabs with a mallet. Throwing back the covers in the morning and hopping out of bed. Running my hands across my husband's chest and feeling it.

One day we shall hear these words uttered that haven't been spoken since Adam was thrust out of Eden: "There shall be no more sorrow."

 Here's my partial list of the benefits of heaven's negatives. Number the benefits from most important to you to least important. Then thank God for each one. As you see, you can even add your own.

___ no more sorrow   ___ no more hunger
___ no more pain   ___ no more thirst
___ no more tears   ___ no more death
___ no more darkness
___ no more separation from God
___ other _____

Next wel

Lesson 4

Where Is Heaven?

As a child I wondered where God lived in outer space and how long it would take to get there. Had I been old enough to read an astronomy textbook, I would have discovered that our solar system has a diameter of about 700 light-minutes. That's eight billion miles. But the galaxy in which our solar system is contained has a diameter of 100,000 light-years. Not minutes, but years. Forget doing the math on that one. Our galaxy is huge. But our galaxy—100,000 light-years wide—is just one of billions of other galaxies out in the cosmos.[3]

I can't comprehend such gargantuan distances nor the breathless enormity of space. Billions of stars and planets, all created by God, most of which the Hubble Space Telescope will never have time to scan. But it's up there on the edge of earth's atmosphere obediently and systematically doing just that — scanning the universe. Hubble has captured images close to the very border of our cosmos. I think it would knock our socks off if it could photograph the actual edge!

 What is on the other side? Complete the margin activity.

Far beyond intergalactic space with its billions of swirling nebulae and novas lies another dimension. Some speculate it's the fifth dimension. You could call it infinity, but wherever it is and however far out, the Bible calls it the highest of heavens. "To the Lord your God belong the heavens, even the highest

Do you think we will ever see heaven with a telescope? Why or why not?

No. It is not something that will be seen by the human eye. Heaven has a spiritual concept

20

heavens"(Deuteronomy 10:14). It would seem this "third heaven," as Scripture calls it, spreads out into infinity and completely engulfs our expanding cosmos with all its celestial bodies.

Let me explain using a principle I learned from high school geometry. If you move a dot through time and space, it makes a line—the first dimension. Take that line, move it laterally through time and space, and it becomes a plane—the second dimension. Move a plane through time and space, and you get a cube or some other polyhedron—a cube is the third dimension and it's comprised of a stack of planes.

You and I, who are three-dimensional figures, move through time and space. We might consider that a fourth dimension. Each new dimension contains the previous ones, plus something more. This means eternity—we might think of it as a fifth dimension—comprises all the interesting elements of the other dimensions, including time.

Hey, if you get that, you get an A in geometry. You also get that time won't stop in heaven but will be swallowed up. The dwelling place of God exists in infinity. I'm amused when the apostle Paul writes so casually in 2 Corinthians 12:2, "I know a man in Christ who fourteen years ago was caught up to the third heaven. Whether it was in the body or out of the body I do not know—God knows. And I know that this man … was caught up to paradise. He heard inexpressible things, things that man is not permitted to tell."

Paul wasn't the only one to reach the throne of heaven in a flash. To the dying thief next to Him on the cross, Jesus said, "I tell you the truth, today you will be with me in paradise" (Luke 23:43).

Heaven Is Spirit-born

As any good child in Sunday School, I believed that heaven was "up." In later years I discovered the Bible says it plainly: Paul was caught up to the third heaven; Jesus ascended into heaven; the Lord will catch us up into heaven when He returns; conversely, "God looks down from heaven on the sons of men" (Psalm 53:2). The Bible invites us to use this language, much as it encourages us to use other earthbound words like "crowns" or "seas of glass."

Distances like "up" and "down" lose their meaning when you realize that heaven—even the highest heavens—exist beyond our space-time continuum. Latitude and longitude, as well as directions and distances are related to time, and time is a part of the fourth dimension. And the fourth dimension is

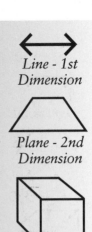

Line - 1st Dimension

Plane - 2nd Dimension

Cube - 3rd Dimension

Time/Motion - 4th Dimension

Heaven exists beyond our space-time continuum.

Line - 1st
Dimension

Plane - 2nd
Dimension

Cube - 3rd
Dimension

Time/Motion
- 4th
Dimension

Heaven -5th
Dimension

only a small part of infinity. Time there will be swallowed up and you enter the fifth dimension where the dying thief, when he died, instantly appeared in paradise alongside Jesus.

The concept of a fifth dimension is difficult to grasp. Think of the transition from the first three dimensions (objects that occupy space) to the fourth dimension (time and thus movement). If you are in the third dimension (you are!), how far away is the fourth dimension?

The fourth dimension comes in to place

Where is the fourth dimension? *when ever I move any self or a bject*

The answer to the questions contain the solution to the other question. How could the dying thief be in paradise instantly? Heaven is all around us. Think of it like this. The fourth dimension (time) is everywhere. We are part of space (the first three dimensions) and we are part of time. Space takes place within time. In the same way, the fifth dimension, the presence of God, is infinitely close and at the same time infinitely far away. Everything we know takes place inside the dimension of heaven—just as everything we can see, smell, or touch takes place within time.

Had I been the dying thief, I would have been dumbstruck to hear Jesus say, "Today, you will be with me in paradise." Today? Like Jesus taking my hand and walking with me through a wall, as He did in the Upper Room? Or appearing on a beach to cook breakfast for His friends? Or ambling along the road to Emmaus and — flash — arriving in Jerusalem in no time flat? Like being changed in the twinkling of an eye?

Yes, and the Lord gives a clue as to how He does it in Revelation 1:8 when He laughs at time and distance: " 'I am the Alpha and Omega,' says the Lord God, 'who is, and who was, and who is to come, the Almighty.' " Notice that Jesus does not follow the convention of our logic about the way time flows; we time-bound creatures want to change the order to read Jesus was, is, and is to come. It sounds more chronological. It's consistent with our sense of the past, present, and future. But Jesus is the great "I Am." He is the God of the now.

I think of this every time I read Revelation 22 when Jesus says three times to the waiting church, "I am coming soon!"

(To which the church replies three times, "Come!") It's interesting He doesn't say, "I will come . . . like, sometime around, oh, a couple of thousand years from now." Jesus puts it in the present tense as though He were but a hairsbreadth away, all ready to part the veil of time and distance and step back into our world. It's as though He were on His way back now.

So the kingdom of heaven, over which Jesus is and was and ever shall be King, is a place, but more so, a dimension where time and distance are not obstacles. The dying thief wasn't transported at superhuman speed to heaven when he died. Rather, he slipped from one dimension to the next, much like Jesus slipped from one room to another through walls.

You cannot be transported to heaven. You cannot go there in a rocket ship. You couldn't even go there in a time machine, if there were such a thing. Heaven exists beyond even speeded-up time. Traveling at a zillion miles per hour might catapult you instantly to the edge of our universe, but to take a step into heaven requires more. It requires something different, for our flesh and blood cannot enter heaven.

 According to John 3:5-7 (margin), what does it take to enter heaven?

You must be born again

You must be born again or you not only can't enter, you cannot even "see the kingdom of God." When the dying thief was born of the Spirit, he was given the spiritual "genes," so to speak, of God Himself—Christ who is, was, and ever shall be. When we are Spirit-born, we, like the thief, are fit for eternity. Of course, we must also follow the dying thief in another way and die first.

Heaven Is Present

Heaven is close. Perhaps closer than we imagine. It's a little like saying to an unborn infant in his mother's womb, "Do you realize you are about to be born into a great big world of mountains, rivers, a sun and a moon? In fact, you exist in that world now."

"Wait a minute," the unborn baby might say. "No way. My world is the one surrounding me. It's soft, warm, and dark. You'll never convince me that just a few hairbreadths outside this uterus exists this place of rivers, mountains, and a sun and moon, whatever that stuff is."

Jesus answered, "I tell you the truth, no one can enter the kingdom of God unless he is born of water and the Spirit. Flesh gives birth to flesh, but the Spirit gives birth to spirit. You should not be surprised at my saying, 'You must be born again.'"
–John 3:5-7

Dear baby! There he is, safe in his little world, ignorant of the fact that a more glorious world is enclosing and encasing his. It is a world for which he is being fashioned. Only when he is birthed into it will he comprehend that all along his warm dark world was within it. This other place of wonderful beauty was present all the time.

 In the margin complete the following analogy, "as the external world is all around the unborn baby, so heaven is..." If you are better with words, write your response. If you are visual, draw a picture to illustrate the idea.

One day we will take the same trip as the dying thief. In the meantime we exist in the kingdom of heaven now. We have already come to Mount Zion, to the heavenly Jerusalem.

We have come to myriad angels in joyful assembly.

We have come to God, the judge of all men. There's a significant part of us, the "new creature in Christ," which lives in the present tense, very much like our great "I Am."

This fact makes the far and distant, near and oh so close. When we seize this reality, we understand that the air we breathe is celestial. The ground we tread is sacred. The light we enjoy is divine.

 Think of the times you have felt alone or abandoned by God. How has this lesson encouraged you to feel God's presence? Write a prayer in the margin expressing your feelings to God about what you have studied.

DO + lesson 2

Lesson 5
How Do I Get to Heaven?

Now faith is being sure of what we hope for and certain of what we do not see.
—*Hebrews 11:1*

Belief in heaven has always been a matter of faith. Stop and pick apart the verse in the margin. Faith means believing in realities that go beyond sense and sight. It is being sure of something you hope for, sure about unfulfilled things in the future. And it's being certain of something you can't see, being aware of unseen divine realities all around you. To put it another way, faith not only makes you sure that heavenly streets of gold really exist, but it helps you see something beyond the earthly streets of asphalt that exist in the here and now.

Now, it takes no more than a mustard seed-sized grain of faith to be sure of unfulfilled things in the future. It takes no great faith to be aware of unseen divine realities all around us. If you are aware of realities you can't see, and if you're certain there are many more realities yet to be fulfilled, you are halfway to solving the mystery!

Let's try it out on a few word pictures in the Book of Ezekiel.

The prophet is sitting by a river bank when suddenly—in a flash—he squints at the heavens opening above him. "I looked, and I saw ... an immense cloud with flashing lightning and surrounded by brilliant light. The center of the fire looked like glowing metal, and in the fire was what looked like four living creatures ... their faces looked like this..." Then Ezekiel goes on to describe four heads with eyes, ears, noses, and mouths of oxen and men, lions and eagles.

My heart goes out to Ezekiel. He was just minding his own business by the river when, without warning, God pressed his eyes smack-flat against the brilliance of heaven, a brilliance that the ordinary faithful see from a distance, and then, only through a glass darkly. The prophet strained to find words to describe what he witnessed, but after hunting through his dictionary for adequate nouns and adjectives to draw a picture of heaven, he had to fall back on language that was old and familiar. Thus, he pictures beasts with weird faces and wheels that science fiction writers would dream up.

Ezekiel courageously plunged ahead and put it into writing. God revealed to him something supernatural—a whole bunch of unseen divine realities—but God didn't give the prophet a thesaurus of supernatural words. So Ezekiel had to rely on the language of resemblance. The center of the fire looked like this ... and the faces looked like that. In fact, the nearer Ezekiel approaches the burning throne, the less sure his words.

You can almost hear Ezekiel stutter and stammer starting with verse 26 of chapter 1.

 As you read Ezekiel's words in the margin, underline each time he compares what he saw to something in his world.

Did you mark all the "looked likes" and "like that ofs" and "what appeared to bes" and "as ifs"? Poor guy. The throne wasn't anything like King David's; the piece of furniture Ezekiel observed was more like "the appearance of a throne." And the

Above the expanse over their heads was what looked like a throne of sapphire, and high above on the throne was a figure like that of a man. I saw that from what appeared to be his waist up he looked like glowing metal, as if full of fire, and that from there down he looked like fire; and brilliant light surrounded him. Like the appearance of a rainbow in the clouds on a rainy day, so was the radiance around him. This was the appearance of the likeness of the glory of the Lord.
—Ezekiel 1:26-28

Lord who was sitting on it? He could only be described as "the likeness of the appearance of a man."[4]

The same is true for the apostle John scrambling to write down his heavenly vision as he sits on the beach on the island of Patmos. Thus, the apostle's best effort to describe what looks like rivers of glass, streets of gold, and gates of pearl.

My point? Were Ezekiel and John sure of what they hoped for? Of course. Were they certain of things they had never seen? You bet. They witnessed far into the future something yet to be fulfilled, and when the Lord pulled back the curtain so they could actually see the unseen realities, they trusted Him to bring it to pass. Their faith about heaven may have been hazy in days gone by, but once their eyes were opened, realities with a small *r* became Realities with a capital *R*.

Ezekiel and John saw their hope. We cannot. And this is why the heavenly song is still an echo. It's a yearning, unfulfilled. A longing that is still an ache. But that's not such a bad thing. We may strain and squint to see heaven through a glass darkly, but Jesus commends the faith of people like you and me in John 20:29 when He says, "Blessed are those who have not seen and yet have believed."

From your Bible read Hebrews 11, often called the "heroes of the faith" chapter. Ask God to develop in you such a capacity for faith.

Faith to Find Your Way Home

Do you see it? Are your eyes of faith focusing better? Or rather, can you hear the faint echoes of some distant heavenly song? It's whispering that heaven will not be an unmaking of all the good things we know, but a new and vastly improved version. Heaven will also be an undoing of all the bad things we know as God wipes away every tear and closes the curtain on pain and disappointment.

I'm going to correct something I wrote earlier.: "There are no words for heaven." It should be, "Heaven is too specific, too real for language."[5] If we've learned anything from the prophet Ezekiel and the apostle John, it's that heaven is real. It's not a state or a condition but a place with streets, gates, walls, and rivers. We are wrong in thinking heaven is wispy, thin, and vaporous. Earth is like withering grass, not heaven.

It takes faith to know the place Jesus has gone ahead to prepare. When God chose to talk about heaven, He did so using the nouns and verbs, syntax and grammar of the Bible. And

Heaven will not be an unmaking of all the good things we know, but a new and vastly improved version.

although He mainly expounded on heaven in highly symbolic books like Ezekiel and Revelation, these symbols are meant to be motivation for our minds and fodder for our faith.

Faith focuses not on the scriptural symbols, but inside and beyond them.

Faith develops the skill of holding onto that heavenly moment.

Faith shows you the way home.

This kind of faith will bring heaven into vivid reality. It will bring into vital contact with your heart the things that people call invisible and distant. It will involve your heart and your eyes. If the apostle Paul were here, he would repeat Ephesians 1:18: "I pray also that the eyes of your heart may be enlightened in order that you may know the hope to which he has called you, the riches of his glorious inheritance in the saints."

Step back for a moment, focus your eyes of faith, and then walk with me into a world you've heard about from your youth but have never seen: heaven. Where is this place called heaven and why is it called "home"? Look with me through a glass darkly, and you just might discover that home is closer—and more real—than you ever thought.

Are You Ready for Heaven?

With all this talk about heaven, you must settle one question. Are you ready for heaven? Have you come to the place in your life that you have given yourself to Jesus Christ and received His free gift—the gift of making you His child? My heart's longing is that you know and enjoy God forever. He is saying, "Come home, come home, ye who are weary, come home."[6] The first step in the right direction to your heavenly home begins with an honest prayer from the heart. If you wish to be certain you're homeward bound to heaven and not hell, then borrow the following words and make them your personal prayer:

Lord Jesus, I realize I have lived my life far from You
And I see now how my sin has separated me from You.
Please come into my life — my heart, mind, and spirit —
And make me the person You want me to be.
Forgive me for living away from You all these years
And help me to turn from my old ways
To Your new and righteous ways.
I invite You to be Lord of my life.
And thank you for the difference You will make. Amen.

Heaven is closer — and more real — than you ever thought.

Step-by-step, you will grow to know Him better and to enjoy Him more.

If this is your prayer, then the next step in the right direction is to find a church where you can share your newfound affection for the Lord Jesus with other like-hearted believers in Him who center their faith around the Bible as God's Word. If you are in a study group, share your decision with your group leader and your group. Step-by-step, you will grow to know Him better and to enjoy Him more.

Review the lessons you have completed this week. Below write at least three things you have discovered about heaven (or maybe ideas you have discovered to be false about heaven.)

1. _____

2. _____

3. _____

In what way has this week's study changed your passion for heaven?

_____

_____

Write a prayer expressing your feelings to God about your work this week.

_____

_____

_____

_____

Unit 2

Who Are We in Heaven?

I've been thinking about my heavenly home for years. Naturally, you can understand why: My earthly body doesn't work. That's one reason I dream about heaven all the time.

I can't say my dreams are Technicolor versions of pearly gates and streets of gold; rather, they're more like rough sketches or dim reflections, as when my "eyes … see the king in his beauty and view a land that stretches afar" (Isaiah 33:17). Like the rolling vista of a Kansas wheat field.

One day the dream will come true.

I still can hardly believe it. I, with shriveled, bent fingers, atrophied muscles, gnarled knees, and no feeling from the shoulders down, will one day have a new body—light, bright, and clothed in righteousness—powerful and dazzling.

Can you imagine the hope this gives someone spinal cord-injured like me? Or someone who is cerebral palsied, brain-injured, or who has multiple sclerosis? Imagine the hope this gives someone who is manic depressive. No other religion, no other philosophy promises new bodies, hearts, and minds. Only in the gospel of Christ do hurting people find such incredible hope.

What You'll Learn in This Unit

In this unit we will explore all of these questions and more: What will our new bodies be like? How will our heart's desires change when we get to heaven? Will we know everything God knows? How will we relate to other people? Will we still know our loved ones? In heaven we will become who we were meant to be all along. The Bible has lots of clues for those who eagerly await His appearing!

Unit Scripture

Listen, I tell you a mystery: We will not all sleep, but we will all be changed—in a flash, in the twinkling of an eye, at the last trumpet. For the trumpet will sound, the dead will be raised imperishable, and we will be changed. —1 Corinthians 15:51-52

Lesson 1

We Will Have New Bodies

*ause and dream with me ...
One day no more bulging middles or balding tops. No varicose veins or crow's-feet. No more cellulite or support hose. Forget the thunder thighs and highway hips. It's the body you've always dreamed of. Fit and trim, smooth and sleek.

I want to break up into giggles right now! Little wonder "we eagerly await a Savior from there [heaven], the Lord Jesus Christ, who, by the power that enables him to bring everything under his control, will transform our lowly bodies so that they will be like his glorious body" (Philippians 3:20–21).

Our lowly bodies will be like His glorious body. Astounding. Like Jesus in His resurrected body, we will have hands and arms, feet and legs. We won't be spirit beings, floating around like angels who have no bodies.

A promise like this, though, almost raises more questions than answers. Does a glorified body translate into glorified digestive systems? What about sleeping? What if we prefer our teeth a little crooked rather than perfect and straight? Will we look the same? And if we do, will we recognize each other? Will my husband be "Ken Tada" and my mother, "Margaret Eareckson"? Will I take a swim with a friend if I wish?

Our lowly bodies will be like His glorious body.

 What one thing do you most look forward to about your resurrected body?

_____

What about people who died in the ocean centuries before whose bodies long ago became fish food? Or people who were blown to smithereens in bomb blasts; or pioneers who perished on the prairies, whose bodies dissolved into dust scattered to the four winds? Will God vacuum up the winds, collect and sort everyone's body particles, and divvy out the correct DNA?

Others have wondered the same. The apostle Paul framed their thoughts in 1 Corinthians 15:35 when he said, "But someone may ask, 'How are the dead raised? With what kind of body will they come?'" Paul then cuts those big scary questions down to size when he says, "How foolish!" In other words, "Guys, get real. Open your eyes." And starting with verse 36, he sketches a few lessons from nature.

Read the verses in the margin. Answer the following true or false according to the passage.

_____ Our resurrection bodies will be just like our present bodies.
_____ Our resurrection bodies will be far greater than our present bodies.
_____ Our resurrection bodies will be related to our present bodies as a full-grown plant is related to a seed.
_____ We will choose the characteristics of our resurrection bodies.

Have you ever seen those nature specials on public television where the camera is put up against a glass to show a dry old lima bean in the soil? Through time-lapse photography, you watch it shrivel, turn brown, and die. Then, miraculously, the dead shell of that little bean splits open and a tiny lima leg-like root sprouts out. The old bean is shoved aside against the dirt as the little green plant swells. The lima plant came to life because the old bean died.

The resulting plant is far greater than the old bean though it comes from it. The bean cannot choose the characteristics of the plant. God determines what our resurrection bodies will be. Answers to the exercise above are false, true, true, and false.

Not even someone with a Ph.D. in Botany can explain how life comes out of death, even in something so simple as a seed. But one thing is for sure: it's a lima bean plant. Not a bush of roses or a bunch of bananas. There's no mistaking it for anything other than what it is. It has absolute identity. Positively, plain as day, a lima bean plant. It may come out of the earth different than when it went in, but it's the same.

So it is with the resurrection body. We'll have absolute identification with our body that died. I will be able to positively recognize my dad as John Eareckson. The "daddy" I meet in heaven will be my dad; he won't be neutered in my eyes, stripped of all the trappings that made him my father. He may come forth from the earth different than when he was buried, but he won't be mistaken for anyone else.

How many of my father's molecules are required to be reassembled before he can be raised? Very little, I suspect. I once read that if all the DNA were collected from the five bil-

What you sow does not come to life unless it dies. When you sow, you do not plant the body that will be, but just a seed, perhaps of wheat or of something else. But God gives it a body as he has determined, and to each kind of seed he gives its own body.
—1 Corinthians 15:36-38

lion or so persons now inhabiting the earth, it would approximate the size of two five-grain aspirin tablets. The "who" you are and the "who" I am is not that big. It's actually very small.[7]

Besides, how much of that old lima bean was the "seed" out of which life miraculously came forth? The best botanists in the world can't answer that one. No one knows how much of that seed is required or even how life can spring from a dead seed. It's one of God's miracles of nature.

So it will be with the resurrection. God will not have to use every part of your body in order to resurrect it. Yet, somehow, the particular person that you are carries on. Jesus gives a simple biology lesson in John 12:24: "I tell you the truth, unless a kernel of wheat falls to the ground and dies, it remains only a single seed. But if it dies, it produces many seeds." The same faith that allows us to believe the harvest is coming enables us to believe in the resurrection.

 Many people believe in the harvest but doubt the resurrection. What would you say to them to affirm your belief in the resurrection of the body?

_____

_____

_____

What Kind of Body?
What about the second question, With what kind of body will they come? True to the apostle Paul and his lessons from nature, all we have to do is open our eyes and look around. "You do not plant the body that will be, but just a seed. If there is a natural body, there is also a spiritual body. And just as we have borne the likeness of the earthly man [Adam], so shall we bear the likeness of the man from heaven [Jesus]" (1 Corinthians 15:37, 44, 49).

Somehow, somewhere within you is the pattern of the heavenly person you will become, and if you want to catch a glimpse of how glorious and full of splendor your body will be, just do a comparison. Compare a hairy peach pit with the tree it becomes, loaded with fragrant blossoms and sweet fruit. They are totally different, yet the same. Compare a caterpillar with a butterfly. A wet, musty flower bulb with an aromatic hyacinth. A hairy coconut with a graceful palm tree.

Within you is the pattern of the heavenly person you will become.

Go on a field trip. Walk around your yard, neighborhood, or garden. Select some plant or tree. Consider the connection between the plant and the seed from which it came. Pray. Talk to God about your desire to be the complete creation He made you to be.

In Luke 4:18 Jesus applied Isaiah 61 to himself. Read Isaiah 61:3 in the margin to see what Jesus said He came to make of you.

No wonder we get stymied thinking about our resurrection bodies, whether or not our teeth will be straight or our digestive systems intact. First Corinthians 15:42-44 (margin) only touches on it. It is sown ... it is raised. We may not be able to describe the changes, but we know it's the same "it." You and what you will one day be are one and the same—yet different.

Trying to understand what our bodies will be like in heaven is much like expecting an acorn to understand its destiny of roots, bark, branches, and leaves. Or asking a caterpillar to appreciate flying. Or a peach pit to fathom being fragrant. Or a coconut to grasp what it means to sway in the ocean breeze. Our eternal bodies will be so grand, so glorious, that we can only catch a fleeting glimpse of the splendor to come.

Lima beans. Kernels of wheat. Peach pits. Acorns and oak trees. The Bible invites us to use examples in nature since "what we will be has not yet been made known" (1 John 3:2).

Can you now see why I enjoy dreaming about heaven?

Since our bodies here on earth are the temple of the Holy Spirit, they have value even though they will be gloriously changed in heaven. Thank God for your earthly body.

They will be called oaks of righteousness, a planting of the Lord for the display of his splendor.
—Isaiah 61:3

The body that is sown is perishable, it is raised imperishable; it is sown in dishonor, it is raised in glory; it is sown in weakness, it is raised in power; it is sown a natural body, it is raised a spiritual body.
—1 Corinthians 15:42-44

Don't you know that you yourselves are God's temple and that God's Spirit lives in you?
—1 Corinthians 3:16

Lesson 2

We Will Have New Hearts

Please don't assume that all I ever do is dream about springing out of this chair, stretching glorified fingers and toes, and pole-vaulting over the pearly gates. However much I relish the idea of leaving this wheelchair behind, that is still, for me, not the best part of heaven.

The best part of heaven will be a completely purified heart.

I can put up with legs and arms that don't obey. Hands that refuse to pick up things no matter how much my mind commands them to move are a fact of life. I can cope with this.

However, there's something with which I can't cope. In fact, the older I get and the closer to heaven I draw, the less I'm able to adjust to it. I am sick and tired of combating my flesh; that is, "the law of sin at work within my members" that just won't do as I command. "When I want to do good, evil is right there with me. For in my inner being I delight in God's law; but I see another law at work in the members of my body, waging war against the law of my mind and making me a prisoner of the law of sin at work within my members. What a wretched man I am!" (Romans 7:21-24).

That's why the best part of heaven will be a completely purified heart. I'm weary of constant confession. I despise sinning. It pains me to keep erring and straying, to do things that I shouldn't do, grieving that I miserably offend the God I love. My heart is soiled and stained, and that drives me to the Lord on my knees (at least, metaphorically). What's odd is, the closer I draw to Jesus, the more intense the heat of the battle.

 Do a heart-check. On a scale of 1 to 10, where 1 means "No, I don't feel that at all," and 10 means "I identify completely," rate how you relate to my feelings:

___4___ I am sick and tired of combating my flesh.
_9/10_ I'm weary of constant confession.
___1___ I despise sinning.
_10_ I grieve that I miserably offend the God I love.

Never do I feel more on the frontline of this battle than when I offer praise to God. Right in the middle of adoring Him in prayer or singing a praise hymn, my heart will start wandering off into some wicked thought. I have to grab my heart by the aorta and jerk it in line time and again!

 Read the cry of the apostle Paul in Romans 7:24-25 in the margin. Describe a time when this battle rages in your life.

Daily and special time Praying, talking to god, trying to do something good

Who will rescue me from this body of death? Thanks be to God— through Jesus Christ our Lord!
—Romans 7:24-25

One day Jesus will come back to complete the salvation He began when I first believed. One day He will release me from the presence and influence of evil. That's why the bad news of Romans chapter 7 is followed by the good news of Romans chapter 8: "We ourselves, who have the firstfruits of the Spirit, groan inwardly as we wait eagerly for our adoption as sons, the redemption of our bodies" (Romans 8:23).

Right here is the highest and most exalted reason that "flesh and blood cannot inherit the kingdom of God" (1 Corinthians 15:50). Entrance to heaven requires a redeemed body. The body must be rid of the law of sin at work in its members. At this present time, the spirit is willing but the flesh is weak. The day is coming, however, when instead of being a hindrance to the spirit, the body will be the perfect vessel for the expression of my glorified mind, will, and emotions. One day we will be "clothed in righteousness," brilliant and glorious.[8]

I can't wait to be clothed in righteousness without a trace of sin. True, it will be wonderful to stand, stretch, and reach to the sky, but it will be more wonderful to offer praise that is pure. I won't be crippled by distractions or disabled by insincerity. I won't be handicapped by a ho-hum halfheartedness. My heart will join with yours and bubble over with effervescent adoration. We will finally be able to fellowship fully with the Father and the Son.

For me, this will be the best part of heaven.

Set Your Hearts on Things Above

The verse in the margin is a command. We may think this command isn't as necessary as other mandates in Scripture, but it is.

 Below write your own paraphrase of the command to "set your heart on things above."

_____

_____

Since, then, you have been raised with Christ, set your hearts on things above, where Christ is seated at the right hand of God.
—Colossians 3:1

When you consider that the first and greatest commandment is to love the Lord with all your heart and mind, it follows that we should set our entire being (that's what it means when it says "heart and mind") on things above.

My heart is the seat of all kinds of appetites and affections. Isn't yours? Our heart is hungry, not for food, but for a whole

range of wrong coordinates. Sometimes the hunger in our heart gets us into trouble, and we wish we could curb the appetites. You'll be surprised, though, to learn who gives us these desires.

 As you read the words of Deuteronomy 8:2-3, underline the reasons God gives for why He causes us to hunger.

Remember how the Lord your God led you all the way in the desert these forty years, to humble you and to test you in order to know what was in your heart, whether or not you would keep his commands. He humbled you, causing you to hunger and then feeding you with manna, which neither you nor your fathers had known, to teach you that man does not live on bread alone but on every word that comes from the mouth of the Lord.
—Deuteronomy 8:2-3

Did you underline the words to teach, humble, and test you to know what was in your heart? The Lord is the one who causes us to hunger. At first, this seems odd. Doesn't God know the "hungries" often get us into trouble?

God has good reasons for placing within us a heart with such burgeoning appetites. He does so to test and humble us, to see what is in our innermost being, to see whether or not we would follow Him. According to Deuteronomy, He places in our sight a whole range of things that could get us off track, but His purpose is never to tempt, only to test to see if we will zero in on the right coordinates. Will you succumb to the handsome face of your best friend's husband or will you choose heaven? Will you covet that third Penn International 50W fishing reel or will you desire heaven? Will you max out four credit cards or will you invest in heaven?

His purpose is to see if we will zero in on the right coordinates.

 What tempts me may not tempt you, but we all have our danger points—those things that call out to us. Below list at least three temptations. Think about some ways to resist temptation that you can share with your group.

1. _____

2. _____

3. _____

To hunger is to be human, but to satiate yourself on God is to send your heart ahead to heaven. Feed on Him in your heart, and you will be yanking that foot out of the mud of earth and stepping closer to eternity.

I admit it's a constant struggle to set our hearts on things above. Always and always we want more. Where we place our citizenship, whether in heaven or on earth, is revealed by those things we passionately desire. If we desire dull, sensual things of earth, our souls reflect that dullness; if our desires rise to find fulfillment in the noble, pure, and praiseworthy, then and only then do we find satisfaction, rich and pleasurable.

The great in the kingdom of heaven will simply be those who set their hearts on Christ and loved Him more. The great will be those who, having received a "You're off course!" warning from the heart's homing detector, simply got back on track.

That's the way I want to live. When I read, "Delight yourself in the Lord and he will give you the desires of your heart" (Psalm 37:4), I want to focus on Jesus, not my heart's list of desires. I realize that curbing the appetites of my heart will heighten my loneliness on earth, but I'm convinced I am destined for unlimited pleasure at the deepest level in heaven. I also know that nothing now quite meets the standards of my yearning heart. This ache drives me to anticipate heaven.

For me, true contentment on earth means asking less of this life because more is coming in the next.

 If I "delight myself" in the Lord, how will that change my desires?

_____

_____

I'm convinced I am destined for unlimited pleasure at the deepest level in heaven.

Godly contentment is great gain. Because God has created the appetites in your heart, it stands to reason that He must be the consummation of that hunger. Yes, heaven will galvanize your heart if you focus your faith not on a place of glittery mansions, but on a Person, Jesus, who makes heaven a home.

 Won't it be glorious to be able to talk to the Father with no hindrances? To have a heart that does not wander, a heart without distractions? End your session today with prayer. Review your work in this lesson. As you do so, talk to Him about your heartaches and dreams.

Lesson 3
We Will Have New Minds

I look forward to heaven because I've got a lot invested there. A new body. A new heart free of sin. But there is another aspect of heaven that intrigues me. A new mind!

First Corinthians 13:12 describes it this way: "Now we see but a poor reflection as in a mirror; then we shall see face to face. Now I know in part; then I shall know fully, even as I am fully known." We will have the mind of Christ. No need to worry about feeling dumb or not knowing the answers. "We will know as we are known," and our present knowledge shall increase beyond belief. What's more, the shine of our best thoughts and memories will be made more resplendent as they are magnified through our new minds.

But what about the sad thoughts left over from earth? In the margin read Isaiah 65:17. This verse, at first, looks like a mistake. Didn't we just read that we will fully know all things? Are bad things excluded?

 Which of the following more nearly describes what Isaiah said about painful memories?

❑ The thoughts will be blotted out.
❑ We won't know about painful events.
❑ We will not need to recall the events.

Our ignorance or imperfect thoughts and memories won't be erased so much as eclipsed, like the stars are mitigated by the rising sun. Something so dazzling is going to happen in the world's finale that its light will obscure every dark memory. We won't forget so much as have no need nor desire to remember. Bad things will not, as Isaiah observes, come to mind, for they will be blocked out by the brilliance of the knowledge of God.

Only good things will come to mind. Our thought processes will no longer connive; we won't devise nasty words or scheme wicked plans. We won't battle against idle daydreams or lustful fantasies. Rather, our thoughts will be gloriously elevated for "when he appears, we shall be like him, for we shall see him as he is" (1 John 3:2).

Behold, I will create new heavens and a new earth. The former things will not be remembered, nor will they come to mind. But be glad and rejoice forever in what I will create.
—Isaiah 65:17

With the mind of Christ we shall "know fully." Not halfway, but fully. While we were on earth, we only sort-of-knew or partially understood "all things that God kept working together for our good" and the good of others, especially in the midst of painful trials. Most of the time, we scratched our heads and wondered how the matted mesh of threads in Romans 8:28 could possibly be woven together for our good. On earth, the underside of the tapestry was tangled and unclear; but in heaven, we will stand amazed to see the topside of the tapestry and how God beautifully embroidered each circumstance into a pattern for our good and His glory.

 Do you know the following old hymn? Sing the words if you do (sing in the shower if you like), and thank the Father that you will "understand it better by and by."

> *Trials dark on every hand, and we cannot understand*
> *All the ways that God would lead us to that blessed promised land;*
> *But He'll guide us with his eye, and we'll follow till we die;*
> *We will understand it better by and by.*
> *By and bye, when the morning comes,*
> *When the saints of God are gathered home,*
> *We will tell the story How we've overcome;*
> *We will understand it better by and by.*[9]

We will lift our hands and glorify God when we see how He used the hundred dollars we sacrificed at the missions conference to reach many hundreds in Brazil. We'll see how many times He engineered the right places and the right moments so that we'd meet just the right people—and the happy marriages and friendships which resulted.

We will understand how everything fit. Everything counted. Nothing was wasted. "The Lord works out everything for his own ends—even the wicked for a day of disaster" (Proverbs 16:4). Every jot and tittle of life will give supreme glory to our all-wise and all-powerful God.

Set Your Minds

Colossians 3:1 is really a double command. We are not only to set our hearts on things above where Christ is seated, but "set [our] minds on things above," as well. That's hard. Our hearts hold a shadow of heaven, but not our minds.

We will stand amazed to see how God beautifully embroidered each circumstance into a pattern for our good and His glory.

It's no surprise God said to Isaiah, "For my thoughts are not your thoughts, neither are your ways my ways. ... As the heavens are higher than the earth, so are my ways higher than your ways and my thoughts than your thoughts" (Isaiah 55:8–9). Somehow, I don't think God stays up at night wondering why they don't standardize electric plugs worldwide.

God's thoughts are higher than ours. And the gap needs to be bridged. My thoughts need to rise to the heavenlies where Christ is seated. This means more than just thinking nice Girl Scout thoughts that are clean and reverent. "Set your minds on things above" means just that: thinking about things above.

Is this all too heavenly minded? No way. When my mind chews on Scripture, faith has something to grow on. To set our minds on Christ means not only the contemplation of the divine in heaven, but the divine on earth.

Think about Jesus and Him alone.

 Contemplate Philippians 4:8. Think about how the verse applies to Christ. Picture Jesus blessing the little children and tell Him in prayer how gracious or kind you think He is, how tender of Him to take a baby out of the arms of its mother, rock it gently, and kiss its cheek. Think about Him tousling the hair of a little boy or taking in His hands the face of a child and blessing her. How do these images make you feel toward Jesus?

Think about Him stopping to notice the bleeding hurt of a woman with a hemorrhage healed by His touch. How tender, how compassionate of Jesus. Think about Him turning a face of steel toward religious phonies and squaring off against sin. How holy and awesome of Jesus. And how changed you are after thinking such thoughts.

 In your Bible read Philippians 2:5-11. Look for reasons to praise Jesus. In the margin write at least three of the reasons you find.

This is where love really builds between you and God. Because He is also thinking about you. Psalm 139:17–18 says, "How precious to me are your thoughts, O God! How vast is

Finally, brothers, whatever is true, whatever is noble, whatever is right, whatever is pure, whatever is lovely, whatever is admirable— if anything is excellent or praiseworthy—think about such things.
—Philippians 4:8

the sum of them! Were I to count them, they would outnumber the grains of sand." The Son makes the Father's thoughts available by stooping to make Himself comprehensible to our pea-sized brains. In the Bible, Jesus has given us His thoughts and we have access to the mind of Christ when we lay hold of Him and His ideas. Only then can we be drawn up to heaven.

 Pause for a time of prayer, seeking to think the Father's thoughts. Tell Him your longing to have the mind of Christ.

Lesson 4

We Will Relate to Others

In heaven we will experience perfect people in perfect fellowship. Heaven's wedding supper of the Lamb will be the perfect party. The Father has been sending out invitations and people have been RSVP-ing through the ages. Jesus has gone ahead to hang the streamers, prepare the feast, and make our mansion ready. Like any party, what will make it sweet is the fellowship.

Fellowship with our glorious Savior and with our friends and family.

There are countless people I'm waiting to see. Queen Esther, Daniel, Jonah, and, of course, Mary and Martha. What's amazing is that I'll immediately recognize these people and all the other redeemed whom I never met on earth. If the disciples were able to recognize Elijah and Moses standing next to Jesus on the Mount of Transfiguration—saints they had never laid eyes on—then the same is true for us. I can't wait to meet them!

 In the margin write the names on your top 10 list. Name 5 people you have known that you look forward to seeing again and 5 people you look forward to meeting for the first time.

One person I'm particularly eager to see in heaven is Steve Estes, my friend whom I mentioned in unit 1. He's a small-town pastor of a country church in Pennsylvania. Next to my husband, he's my dearest friend. Ken is the first to understand and accept my affection for Steve. After all, Ken realizes that in

the sixties the Lord used this young man to lift me out of my suicidal despair. Steve understood nothing about wheelchairs, but he loved Christ with a passion. He wanted me—his depressed neighbor fresh out of the hospital—to find help and hope in God's Word. So we made an arrangement: I provided plenty of cola and he came to my house on Friday nights with his Bible to help me painstakingly piece together the puzzle of my suffering. Yes, I found the help and hope he talked about. And the rest is history.

That was a long time ago, and even though we only visit occasionally over the phone, our friendship remains strong and secure. Still, whenever I miss "the good ol' days" or wish I could see him more often, these longings are tempered by one amazing thought: We shall be forever friends.

Our friendship is no coincidence. God has something eternal in mind for me and Steve. How do I know? In Acts 17:26 it says, "From one man he made every nation of men, that they should inhabit the whole earth; and he determined the times set for them and the exact places where they should live."

Did you catch that? Of all the billions of possibilities, of all the millions of people with whom I could be friends, the Lord chose Steve for me. A few more miles between our houses, or a few more years between our ages, and chances are we would never have encountered each other. But for Christians there are no such chances. "Christ who said to the disciples, 'You have not chosen me, but I have chosen you,' can truly say to every group of Christian friends, 'You have not chosen one another but I have chosen you for each other.'"[10]

 Do you have one friend who has stuck with you through the years—maybe even from long distance? What circumstances brought you together? Pray now for that person, and thank God for providing this friend.

Such a view of friendship has powerful implications for eternity. Friendship initiated on earth barely has time to get started; we only scratch its surface in the few short years we reside here. Its greater and richer dimension will unfold in heaven. God has a plan for Steve and me in eternity and together we will play an intimate role in carrying out that special plan. I will love him as I never thought possible on earth. Wow, if I think my husband, and Steve, and others that I hold dear bring me joy in the here and now, just think what's in store for us in heaven!

For Christians there are no chance encounters.

How it will pan out is yet to be seen, but this I know: All the earthly things we enjoy with our friends here will find their more exalted expression in heaven. We will do things with our friends for the sheer joy of being together and blessed by God.

Heavenly fellowship with friends won't be some ethereal do-nothingness where we yawn, sit around on clouds, and ogle at angels. Oh, the things we shall do! You and your friends will rule the world and judge the angels. Together, friends will eat the fruit of the tree of life and be pillars in the temple of God. Together, we shall receive the morning star and be crowned with life, righteousness, and glory. Most of all, together we shall fall on our faces at the foot of the throne and worship our Savior forever.

Note how many times I've used the word "together." Heaven is by no means a hangout for mavericks roaming the universe and doing their own thing. It's a place of sweet togetherness and maybe that's why it says we all live in a city, the New Jerusalem. We won't be speckled here and there in rural cottages isolated from one another, but we'll live in harmony in a city. A nice city. A holy city!

Dreaming about this city makes missing Steve—and many other dear friends—more bearable. It even makes my relationship with friends who have died and gone on to glory sweet and close.

The same is true for you. Read Acts 17:26 again and rejoice that it's no accident that you are living in this decade, in your part of the country, and in your town where you enjoy your best friends. These dear ones in your life are no coincidence. You could have been born in another time and place, but God determined to "people" your life with these particular friends.

These special ones strike a resonant chord in your heart; there is something about them, some aspect of beauty or goodness that reminds you of God. I have an inkling that when you see the face of God in heaven, you will say, "Yes, I always knew You!" It was Him all along that you loved whenever you were with that treasured person. In friendship, God opens your eyes to the glories of Himself, and the greater the number of friends with whom you share deep and selfless love, the better and clearer the picture of God you will have.

 In the margin write a characteristic of God that you have come to appreciate through seeing it lived out in your friends.

From one man he made every nation of men, that they should inhabit the whole earth; and he determined the times set for them and the exact places where they should live.
—Acts 17:26

I tell you, there is rejoicing in the presence of the angels of God over one sinner who repents.
—Luke 15:10

We will worship with the angels.

How Will We Relate to Angels?

One of the best parts of heaven may be getting to know and fellowship with angels. They love God and they enjoy us. In a parable about sinners gaining entrance into the kingdom of heaven, Jesus gave us a clear picture of how the angels feel about us.

If angels rejoiced so happily over our conversion, how much more will they rejoice over us when we arrive at the foot of God's throne. To the angels, we will be a source of eternal joy. They will see our redemption completed, from beginning to end.

We will also worship with the angels. They've had a lot of practice at worshiping, as well as access to heaven's throne. They've seen it all. Yet when we arrive in heaven, it will be their privilege to worship with us. Just think what our worship will sound like. In Revelation 5:11-12, angels crowd before the throne, "numbering thousands upon thousands, and ten thousand times ten thousand. . . .. In a loud voice they sang: 'Worthy is the Lamb, who was slain, to receive power and wealth and wisdom and strength and honor and glory and praise!' "

Every time I read that verse, I recall a marvelous experience at the Moody Pastor's Conference. I was told that the singing would be out of this world, and it was. The song leader had the men stand up. When they held hymnbooks high and broke into a rousing chorus, a jet blast of sound hit me head-on. Something forced me to close my eyes and just listen.

Never had I been so utterly surrounded by sound. It was pure and powerful, clear and deep, resonating through my bones, and shaking the chair in which I sat. A thunderous waterfall of perfect bass and baritone, so passionate it made my heart break. It was a moment of ecstasy, so serendipitous and God-anointed, that I had to step outside myself and be carried heavenward. I could do nothing but laugh through my tears and enjoy the ride. If this earthly choir moved me, how much more when our voices blend with the angels!

 Review this lesson. Of the promises about heaven, which realization thrills you most?

- ❏ I will have a body with all working parts.
- ❏ I will have all the time in the world with loved ones.
- ❏ I will understand why so many things happened.
- ❏ I will get to know the angels who have watched over me.
- ❏ Other _____

Lesson 5

We Will Receive Our True Identity

*T*hat we have not understood or lived out our true identity is a basic tragedy of life. Our lost youth and lost identity are not to be recovered in the innocence of Eden. God conceived of us before Eden, "before the foundation of the world." Only in heaven—the birthplace of our identity—will we find out who we truly are. Actually, we won't find it so much as receive it. This is beautifully symbolized in Revelation 2:17: "To him who overcomes, I will give some of the hidden manna. I will also give him a white stone with a new name written on it, known only to him who receives it."

Did you get that part about our new name? George MacDonald explains the connection between our new name and our true identity this way: "God's name for a man must be the expression of his own idea of the man, that being whom he had in his thought when he began to make the child, and whom he kept in his thought through the long process of creation which went to realize the idea. To tell the name is to seal the success."[11]

Your true identity will unfold in the new name God will give you. The name is a secret between God and you. Think about that, friend! In heaven you will not only find what was irretrievably lost, but when you receive it—your new name, your true identity—you will be a thousand times more yourself than the sum total of all those nuances, gestures, and inside subtleties that defined the earthbound "you." On earth you may think you fully blossomed, but heaven will reveal that you barely budded.

What's more, you will be like none other in heaven. The fact that no one else has your name shows how utterly unique you are to God. You touch His heart in a way no one else can. You please Him like none other. It is a royal seal of His individual love on you.

This shouldn't surprise us. God hasn't carved out a gigantic celestial ballpark called heaven into which His entire family fits. Paradise is not a general commune for a lump sum of saints. You have a specific place niched in heaven—in God's heart—which fits you and you alone. In heaven you will reflect Him like a facet of a diamond. People will say to you, "I love

You have a specific place niched in heaven—in God's heart—which fits you and you alone.

45

seeing that part of God in you ... in fact, you show off that trait of His better than anybody up here!"

I know that you have felt misunderstood sometimes; we all have. Other people fail to recognize you for the unique person God made you to be. Examples range from being blamed for something you wouldn't do to being pushed into a lifetime vocation you did not choose.

 Think of a major time in your life when you felt misunderstood. In the margin write a few words to describe the situation. What difference does it make to know that someday you will be fully understood and appreciated for who you uniquely are?

Everyone else will receive their true identity too. They also will reflect God in unique and complete ways; so you will probably say to that friend, "Well, I love the way you reflect Him this way!" And together the two of you, as well as all the other saints, will praise God that He is "all and in all" with such variety and beauty.

C. H. Spurgeon suggested this is why redeemed people will number more than the grains of sand on the beach or the stars in the sky. An endless number of saints will be required to fully reflect the infinite facets of God's love. Everyone is necessary in heaven. Could it be that without you, some wonderful nuance of God's love, dare I say, might not get reflected were you not in heaven?

 How do you react to the idea that you are an important facet of God's love? Place a dot on the continuum below:

Applies to someone else   *Pleased and honored*

We will finally and fully discover who we are, where we belong, and what God destined us to do.

United in perfect praise and love, we will finally and fully discover who we are, where we belong, and what God destined us to do—and we will have all of eternity to be and do that very thing.

You will recognize the ones you love. On earth you only half-recognized them. But in heaven, you will discover rich, wonderful things about the true identity of your husband, wife, daughter, son, brother, sister, or special friends, things that were only hinted at on earth. What's more, you will know them like you never knew them on earth. After all, we won't be less smart in heaven, we will be smarter. My husband Ken will be a thousand times more "Ken" than he ever was in flesh and blood. You will exclaim to your loved one, "Wow, so this is what I loved in you for so long!" for you will see him or her as God intended all along.

Perfection of Body and Soul

Perfection of body and soul can, to some, sound boring.

I have two friends, John and Mike. They are wonderful brothers in Christ, but they are the robust sort who would rather tackle the work of the kingdom on earth and not get sidetracked with future things. They'll do their God-appointed job here and let heaven take care of itself. Anyway, their picture of heaven is static—a never ending do-nothingness in which there are no more things to achieve or goals to accomplish. For them, heaven is literally the end. The idea of a "never-ending relationship at the feet of Jesus," though comforting, doesn't get them charged.

Perfection? Nah, they savor the spice of a good argument now and then. "Who wants a friend, or even a wife, who always agrees with you?" they say.

These guys would rather help pave the streets of gold with titanium monster trucks, back loaders, and steamrollers. They'll take kayaking on the River of Life any day, and would rather take Joseph and Daniel fly-fishing than sit around and listen to them explain dream therapy.

I'm not about to fault these friends of mine. Frankly, I hope they take me fly-fishing as well. They're just being left-brained. They're into logic and explanations and—watch it—clunky earthly symbols. Perfection of body and soul has nothing to do with casting the perfect fly or playing the perfect round of golf. We can't construct heaven with the Lincoln Logs of our logic. We can't forget that what we imagine turns clunky when we rely on earthly images.

To appreciate the perfection of our bodies and souls, we have to begin to get our hearts and minds somewhat in tune for heaven. Heaven is a prepared place for prepared people. Otherwise, heaven is a turnoff.

It's like this. I love listening to Mozart. That's because Mozart was a master at composing perfect music. I'm told that he arranged his notes flawlessly in every bar of every page and even employed certain numerical progressions that reflect absolute order and symmetry in tone and balance. Mathematicians study this composer. His compositions are perfect.

Heaven is a prepared place for prepared people.

Now if I were to play his "Magic Flute" for a couple of homeboys from my husband's high school, they'd guffaw and turn up the volume on their boom box. Hip-hop and death-rap is more their speed. But it's a far, far cry from perfect music. You have to spend a lot of time listening to perfect music before you can appreciate it.

My point? You have to spend time doing the "be ye perfect as I am perfect" thing here on earth before you can enjoy the idea of heavenly perfection. To John and Mike this, at first, may chill rather than awaken their desire for heaven. But whether left-brained or right-brained, whether macho or meditative, each of us must never avert our eyes from those elements of heaven that seem puzzling or repellent; for it is precisely the puzzlement of perfection that conceals what we do not yet know and yet need to know.

 Check the following ways you are actively pursuing "be ye perfect" in this life:

___ regular prayer   ___ financial stewardship
___ getting rid of a bad habit   ___ witnessing
___ hearing the Word taught   ___ fellowship with
     and preached   other Christians

The closer we draw to the Lord Jesus and the more we set our hearts and minds on heavenly glories above, the better prepared we shall be for heaven's perfection. Fellowship won't mean sitting at the feet of Jesus and fighting back boredom while everyone else is enraptured. No. Fellowship will be the best of what earthly friendship merely hinted at.

I would like to tell John and Mike, "Hey, don't forget, Christ knows better than you what it means to be human. He sailed on the seas, hiked mountains, and slept under the stars by a rushing brook. He realizes what gets your heart pumping. Remember, He made you. You won't stop being human. Rather, you'll enjoy the full richness of all that your humanity was designed to be. You, with all your propensity for chumming it up around the campfire, will be a better ... you!"

And a better you is a perfect you.

 Review the lessons you have completed this week. Write at least three things you have discovered about heaven (or maybe ideas you have discovered to be false about heaven).

I have discovered about heaven...

1. _____

2. _____

3. _____

In what way has this week's study changed your passion for heaven?

_____

_____

Write a prayer expressing your feelings to God about your work this week.

_____

_____

_____

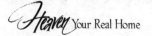
Unit 3
What Will We Do in Heaven?

I take heaven seriously. I take it as seriously as do children. One morning while I was waiting in an airport, I told my five-year-old friend, Matthew Fenlason, and his little brother, Stephen, to grab hold of the arm of my wheelchair and come with me to look for some kids with whom we could play. We found a couple of little boys sitting with their parents in the waiting area. I asked if they would like to play a game with us. Within minutes, in the open area of the airport lounge, we started a game of Duck-Duck-Goose. When Matthew tagged me "goose," I raced in my wheelchair around the circle of children, but I couldn't catch him. Feeling badly that I wasn't able to get up and run, he whispered, "Don't worry, Joni, when we get to heaven your legs will work, and we'll be able to really play Duck-Duck-Goose."

He meant it. And so did I.

It's easy for me to "be joyful in hope," as it says in Romans 12:12, and that's exactly what I've been doing for the past twenty-odd years. My assurance of heaven is so alive that I've been making dates with friends to do all sorts of fun things once we get our new bodies. Rana Leavell and I plan to climb mountains. Thad Mandsager and I, both quads, will snow ski. I want to take a whole circle of Romanian orphans picnicking. And I can't wait to put my friend Judy Butler on a really fast horse and go racing across the fields.

I don't take these appointments lightly. I'm convinced these things will really happen. Think of the pleasure we will experience to see each other sin-free with glowing bodies all light and bright. It will be the answer to all our longings.

What You'll Learn in This Unit

In this unit we will explore more questions about heaven. What about rewards? judgment? What will it be like to praise God forever? In what capacities will we serve God? Just think! You will rule with Him!

Unit Scripture

Father, I want those you have given me to be with me where I am, and to see my glory, the glory you have given me because you loved me before the creation of the world. —John 17:24

Lesson 1

We Will Be Rewarded

*H*eaven will not only be the answer to our longings but those of Jesus as well. You are the fulfillment of His desire. You can hear the yearning in Jesus' voice in John 17:24: "Father, I want those you have given me to be with me where I am, and to see my glory, the glory you have given me because you loved me before the creation of the world." My heart glows to think of His delight when He sees us dressed in white raiment for the wedding supper.

Many of us have a distorted picture of how Jesus sees us and feels about us. Do you tend to think that He looks at you with love and approval—that you give Him pleasure—or that Jesus looks at you with a feeling of disgust?

 Place an X on the scale below to indicate how you tend to think God feels about you.

Disapproval   *Approval*

Scripture clearly teaches that God loves us with an unconditional and everlasting love. Unfortunately, we often do not believe He takes pleasure in us.

In fact, you give Jesus so much pleasure, that somewhere in the midst of the royal heavenly celebration—maybe right before the banquet or soon after—Jesus will rise, ascend His throne, and present rewards and crowns to all the guests. This is a most unusual celebration. It is not the guests who come bearing gifts, but the Host. The Lord Jesus does all the gift giving.

And these rewards aren't your average party favors. We shall be given crowns.

In the margin read 2 Timothy 4:8. The verse reads like the invitation to a coronation. Wow, God wants to award me a crown! Maybe some adults pooh-pooh the idea of rewards, but I don't. The child in me jumps up and down to think God might actually award me something. Nothing is so obvious in a heavenly minded child of God as his undisguised pleasure in receiving a reward—a reward that reflects the approval of the

There is in store for me the crown of righteousness, which the Lord, the righteous Judge, will award to me on that day—and not only to me, but also to all who have longed for his appearing.
—2 Timothy 4:8

Father. So, for all the children whom Jesus said were best fit for the kingdom of heaven, get ready for God to show you not only His pleasure, but His approval.

What does a crown in heaven look like?

 Read Psalm 149:4, appearing in the margin. Check the response below to indicate what the passage tells you about heavenly crowns.

> ❑ Crowns are literal, made of gold and jewel encrusted.
> ☑ Crowns may represent something about our relation-ship with Christ.

The Lord takes delight in his people; he crowns the humble with salvation.
—Psalm 149:4

Psalm 149:4 gives a hint as to what kind of crown God means. God probably doesn't mean a literal crown, because salvation isn't something you put on your head. Heavenly crowns must represent something He does, something He gives, as when He crowns us with salvation. This crown is more resplendent and illustrious than any old hunk of platinum with a lot of sparkly things in it.

 In the following paragraphs, circle each type of crown you see mentioned. As you do so, pray. Thank God for giving you the crown, ask Him to help you understand the crown, or ask Him to give you the wisdom, courage, and commitment required to receive the crown.

The crown of life in James l:12 is reserved for those who per-severe under trials. This means God awards us with life eternal.

God gives the crown of rejoicing in 1 Thessalonians 2:19 to believers who introduce others to Christ. This means He awards us with joy that lasts forever.

The incorruptible crown in 1 Corinthians 9:25 is presented to those who are found pure and blameless on the judgment day. Nothing God gives will ever perish, spoil, or fade.

In l Peter 5:2-4 the crown of glory is reserved for Christian leaders who have guided others. God awards us glory that will never diminish, but only increase.

My favorite, the crown of righteousness mentioned in 2 Tim-othy 4:8, is for those who are itching to have Jesus come back. God will award us this crown because of a lifetime of rightly relating to Him.

Did you circle five crowns in the paragraphs above?

Get ready for crowns!

What About Envy in Heaven?

May I straighten out one thing? I didn't dream up the idea of some people becoming greater in the kingdom than others, Scripture did. One of the last things Jesus says in Revelation 22:12 is, "Behold, I am coming soon! My reward is with me, and I will give to everyone according to what he has done." If you're faithful in a few things, watch out, it's "ten cities" coming your way. If it's a couple of talents you invest, lo and behold, the Master more than doubles your investment. God's Word is replete with conditional statements like, "Blessed is the man who perseveres under trial, because when he has stood the test, he will receive the crown of life" (James 1:12).

As far as envy is concerned, don't worry. It won't happen in heaven. Remember, we will be totally transformed. Envy will be an impossibility. We won't drool over someone's three-story mansion and think we only live in a shack with a tin roof. No competing and no comparison in heaven. It makes perfect sense that God will exalt those whom He chooses to honor. It's His prerogative. And whatever He decides or whomever He chooses to lift up is fine with me. I'll be more than happy for the godly men and women whom Christ will elevate as the most celebrated pillars in His temple.

Yes, some will be greater in the kingdom than others. What a wonderful thought! I can't wait for the Lord to greatly honor the missionary in the back jungles of Brazil who spent 15 years translating Scripture and then quietly moved on to the next tribe.

I want to see the Lord richly reward small-town pastors who faithfully preached every Sunday morning despite meager numbers in the pews. I hope the Lord takes highest delight in elderly grandmothers in nursing homes who didn't dwell on their plight, but rather prayed for others without fanfare. And moms and dads of handicapped children who, in the name of Jesus, served the family faithfully despite the day-to-day routine, isolation, and financial setbacks.

Who would you be thrilled to see the Lord honor? Possibly the person who told you about Jesus? A leader you admire? A missionary? Someone with a servant heart? How about calling those persons or writing a note to tell them of your love and appreciation?

These are the heroes and heroines over whom we will be exceedingly glad to hear the Lord say, "Well done, good and faithful servant!" When they receive their rewards, I'll stand

There will be no competing and no comparison in heaven.

1) you have a new heart
2) I will be just pleased to be in his presant
3) I am thankful for what God has given me in the past?
4)

happily on the sidelines, cheering, whistling, and applauding wildly.

I won't be jealous of others. You won't be either.

 Do you know why you will be satisfied with the reward Jesus gives you? In the margin jot down as many reasons as you can think of why you won't be envious in heaven.

I noted these reasons: first, I'll be pleased with whatever Jesus bestows simply because He's Lord. Second, my sense of justice will be in complete accord with the Lord's judgment. Third, my capacity for joy will be filled to overflowing.

Your reward will be your capacity—your capacity for joy, service, and worship. Jonathan Edwards described these capacities this way: "The saints are like so many vessels of different sizes cast into a sea of happiness where every vessel is full: this is eternal life, for a man ever to have his capacity filled. But after all, 'tis left to God's sovereign pleasure, 'tis his prerogative to determine the largeness of the vessel."[12]

When I think of my vessel, I picture a gallon bucket into which the Lord will pour His joy until it gushes over the brim, bubbling up and effervescing. I'll laugh with delight for others who will have a joy-capacity the size of a big bath tub, or a tanker truck, or a silo. Like me, they will be filled to overflowing.

Motivation for Now

So, I'm fixing my eyes on Jesus and focusing on things unseen. I'm stretching my heart's capacity for God here on earth to prepare my bucket for joy in heaven. I'm searching high and low in my heart to choose the right building materials, whether it be gold, silver, precious stones, or platinum-plated service. I'm down here on earth to receive as many crowns as possible.

Uh-oh, you may be thinking, Joni, aren't you being self-serving here? Isn't focusing on gaining rewards a bit mercenary?

No. I have a clear conscience in light of 1 Corinthians 9:24.

 Read 1 Corinthians 9:24-26 in the margin. Below paraphrase what the verse instructs us to do regarding heavenly rewards.

Jesus is my focus and I will follow his direction, He is my focus and I will work hard at it

Do you not know that in a race all the runners run, but only one gets the prize? Run in such a way as to get the prize. Everyone who competes in the games goes into strict training. They do it to get a crown that will not last, but we do it to get a crown that will last forever. Therefore I do not run like a man running aimlessly; I do not fight like a man beating the air.
—1 Corinthians 9:24-26

Is it selfish to run hard in order to gain the prize? Is working toward rewards mercenary? Certainly not. Heavenly crowns are more than rewards for a job well done on earth; if your focus is on Jesus, they are the glorious fulfillment of the job itself. A reward is the cherry and whipped-cream topping of the pleasure of serving God down here on earth. It is the joy of sticking to the call He gave at the beginning.

Heaven is one big reward. Gift after gift after gift.

 Check the response that most nearly represented your attitude about rewards before you began this study.

☒ I was excited about earning all the rewards possible.
☒ I didn't think about heavenly rewards.
❑ I thought the idea of heavenly rewards was wrong and selfish.
❑ Other _____

If this lesson has changed your attitude about rewards, tell how.

This lesson brought more clarity regarding rewards

Lesson 2

We Will Be Judged

Uh-oh, read 2 Corinthians 5:10 in the margin. All of a sudden this doesn't sound like a coronation celebration. This sounds scary. Especially the "whether good or bad" part. Surely the party will turn sour once everyone sees all the bad things you did on earth. They'll wave you off and groan, "Now I know what he was really like. Boy, am I disappointed!"

Back in high school I used to feel the same about heaven. I never could understand why Christians longed to go there. To me, heaven was a place where not only God would know all and see all, but my friends and family would too. Upon passing through the pearly gates, I saw myself standing under a marquee of a theater: *Now Showing: The Uncensored Version of*

We must all appear before the judgment seat of Christ, that each one may receive what is due him for the things done while in the body, whether good or bad.
—2 Corinthians 5:10

Joni. I pictured myself walking down the aisle and passing people I respected, like my ninth-grade teacher, my hockey coach, and my Sunday School leader. On each aisle I spotted others like the handicapped boy in school I made fun of and the girl down the street I beat up in a fistfight. I pictured reaching the first row, sinking into a seat, and cringing as God then rolled the movie of my life for all to gawk at. Talk about guilt and judgment!

 Read Luke 12:3 in the margin. If this were your idea of the judgment, how would you feel about your secrets being made known?

❏ About like you described—scared to death!
❏ I don't think I'd have much to worry about.
❏ I'd just try not to think about it.
❏ Other _____

I'm inclined to believe that the real judgment seat of Christ will be quite different. Consider 1 Corinthians 4:5: "Therefore judge nothing before the appointed time; wait till the Lord comes. He will bring to light what is hidden in darkness and will expose the motives of men's hearts. At that time each will receive his praise from God."

 What does the verse say God will reveal?

❏ The sordid details of our worst deeds.
❏ The hidden motives of our hearts.

The verse says the Lord will reveal the motives of our hearts. Maybe He knows that I need to come completely face-to-face with the selfishness of my own heart so I can fully appreciate the salvation He provides.

Read the verse one more time. After exposing the motives of our hearts, each will receive "his praise from God." When Christ ascends His throne and sits at the judgment seat, I don't believe He'll roll an uncut, uncensored version of your life. He won't wear the scowl of a rigid and inflexible judge who bangs the gavel and reads aloud your sins for the court record. No, that already happened at another judgment, the judgment at the cross. It was there the Father slammed down the gavel and pronounced His Son "Guilty!" as He became sin for us. It went on record in the courts of heaven and then the indictment was

What you have said in the dark will be heard in the daylight, and what you have whispered in the ear in the inner rooms will be proclaimed from the roofs.
—Luke 12:3

canceled with the words "Paid in Full," written not with red ink, but red blood. Anyway, "If you, O Lord, kept a record of sins, O Lord, who could stand? But with you there is forgiveness; therefore you are feared" (Psalm 130:3-4).

Your sins will not condemn you in heaven.

 Below write your own paraphrase of Psalm 103:10-12 that appears in the margin.

_____

_____

If you have placed your trust in Christ for having borne your transgressions on His cross, then you have nothing to fear. He did away with it. Erased it. Sin no longer has power to wound or to inflict remorse and regret.

 Have you thanked your Heavenly Father today for the indescribable gift He has given you? The one good your past sins serve may be to remind you just how great His salvation really is. Reflect for a moment on God's work in your life. Then tell Him how you feel.

Reward: Greater Capacity for Service

The judgment seat of Christ is different. It's not a trial to determine whether you are guilty or innocent, it is more like a judging stand to ascertain your capacity to serve God.

The following analogy is very simple, but I like to picture a judge's stand at a housing contractor's convention where rewards are distributed to all the architects, builders, foremen, and construction crews. The judge examines the quality of each man's work. Each receives praise for what he has built and how he has built it—praise, not condemnation. It's true that the praise doled out to some contestants will be greater than others, but each will receive his reward. And the prize? The judge will say, "Well done! You've accomplished much with these few buildings, now we will put you in charge of a big development."

Thus, the architects and foremen are awarded larger and more elaborate contracts. And the builders get to roll up their sleeves and tackle the newest and best homes on the market. Each person walks away from the convention happy, heartened, and with an increased capacity to serve the industry.

He does not treat us as our sins deserve or repay us according to our iniquities. For as high as the heavens are above the earth, so great is his love for those who fear him; as far as the east is from the west, so far has he removed our transgressions from us.
—Psalm 103:10-12

I'm constructing with an eye toward eternity.

While we're on earth, we have a chance to "lay up treasures in heaven" and to send ahead, so to speak, building materials so that something of eternal worth can be constructed. That's why "each one should be careful how he builds. For no one can lay any foundation other than the one already laid, which is Jesus Christ. If any man builds on this foundation using gold, silver, costly stones, wood, hay, or straw—his work will be shown for what it is, because the Day will bring it to light. It will be revealed with fire, and the fire will test the quality of each man's work. If what he has built survives, he will receive his reward. If it is burned up, he will suffer loss; he himself will be saved, but only as one escaping through the flames" (1 Corinthians 3:10-15).

I'm constructing with an eye toward eternity, and so can you. Every day we have the opportunity to roll up our spiritual sleeves and apply our spiritual energies toward building something that lasts, in our lives and the lives of others. We are warned to be careful and choose as our building materials gold, silver, and costly stones.

 What can you do to lay up treasure in heaven? Make a list of activities that would fall under the appropriate heading:

Gold, silver, precious stones   Wood, hay, stubble

_____   _____

_____   _____

_____   _____

_____   _____

I believe gold, silver, and precious stones describe service rendered out of a pure heart, a right motive, and an eye for God's glory. On the other hand, wood, hay, or straw describe things done out of an impure motive and an eye to our own glory.

At the Judgment Seat

We will bring to the judgment seat of Christ all that we are and all that we've done. One look from the Lord will scrutinize the quality of what we've built, and selfish service will be consumed in a fiery flash. Although it's true that no child of God will be scolded, some will walk away scalded from the heat; their only reward will be their eternal salvation.

But hey, even if a lot of people survive the judgment seat by the skin of their teeth, keeping only their crown of salvation, that's plenty of cause for rejoicing. Look at all the people who trusted Christ on their deathbed with barely time to say yes to Jesus, let alone build anything for eternity. Think of being snatched from the jaws of hell seconds before one dies. Such joy would be hard to beat.

One look from the Lord will consume worthless service. But it will illuminate God-honoring service. Like gold and precious stones, pure service will easily survive the test. We shall be commended. We will drop to our knees in front of the judgment seat with the words of our Master from Matthew 25:23, 29 ringing in our hearts. Read them in the margin.

 Close your eyes and picture God speaking those words to you. If you don't already have a practice of Scripture memory, begin to memorize and meditate on verses like these, verses that can motivate you to love God more.

I'm dying to hear those words. Literally. I want to put to death every selfish motive and prideful pretense so that when the Lord's eyes scan my service, what I have built will stand the test. I want to be careful how I build and realize that apart from Him, I can do nothing (John 15:5). Every smile, prayer, or ounce of muscle or money sacrificed is a golden girder, brick, or two-by-four. I want everything I do here to be an eternal investment, a way of building something bright and beautiful there. That's how much things down here count.

And no one will be left out. Each will receive his reward. Each of us will have something to do.

 So far in this unit, we've talked about being rewarded and being judged. Describe your feelings now about the prospect of these events.

rewarded _____

_____

judged _____

_____

Well done, good and faithful servant! You have been faithful with a few things; I will put you in charge of many things. Come and share your master's happiness! For everyone who has will be given more, and he will have an abundance.
—Matthew 25:23,29

Lesson 3

We Will Worship and Praise God

Heaven is a place of eternal, loving worship. Our service will be to continually praise God without interruption.

"Huh?" I can just hear my guy friends say. "I'm all for it, but isn't this going to get a little tedious after a while? Won't we run out of Scripture choruses and praise songs after a few millennia?"

I used to feel the same about heaven. Anything changeless had a high boredom factor. Even a great vacation at the beach had a hidden potential to be boring if it went on too long. I was always happy for good things to come to an end after a time.

But in heaven, praise will never become boring.

The only reason we find even the best things monotonous after a while is because of ... a while. In other words, because of the passage of time. Eternity is not changelessness (which is boring) because changelessness means that time passes while everything stays the same. Eternity is not many millennia. It's not even a billion millennia or a trillion. Time doesn't pass in heaven, it just is.

I can hear my macho friends retort, "Yeah, but you can only be enthralled over truth, goodness, beauty, and purity for so long. There's something stifling about arriving at perfection!"

You could only say this if you conceive of truth, goodness, or even eternity as static and abstract. It's not. Truth and goodness, eternity and heaven—yes, God Himself—are not static, but dynamic. Not abstract, but concrete. More real than anything we have ever touched or tasted on earth. Remember, we are wrong in thinking heaven is wispy, thin, and vaporous. Earth is like withering grass, not heaven.

 Read John 20:26 in the margin. Below check the response indicating how you think Jesus had the uncanny ability to walk through earthly walls unobstructed.

❑ Jesus is thin and vaporous—spirit—so He can pass through solid walls.
❑ Jesus is the one who is really solid; earthly matter is vaporous compared to Him.
❑ Other _____

A week later his disciples were in the house again, and Thomas was with them. Though the doors were locked, Jesus came and stood among them and said, "Peace be with you!"
—John 20:26

The question is a matter of speculation, but I believe the second response is true. Jesus and heaven are more real, more substantial, than things of earth. I note that in the very next verse Jesus invited Thomas to touch and feel Him.

Just as Jesus is solid, praise in heaven will have substance. We shall eat from the tree of life.

Taste hidden manna like honey.

Smell truth like a flower.

Wear righteousness like light.

Hold the morning star like a scepter.

Shine like the stars of the heavens.

Enter into the joy of the Lord.

There's nothing inert or abstract about those verbs.

 Be a kid—I recommend it. Invent your own actions to picture the things we will do. For example, "taste hidden manna" could be licking an ice cream cone. Make your actions as wacky as you like. You're a kid, remember? Now act one of them out, and tell God how glad you are to have Him for your Dad.

Everything in heaven will have more substance than we ever dreamed. We will no longer desire our God who is absent, but rejoice in our God who is present.

Why We Will Praise Him Forever

Our worship of God will never end. I compare it to the excitement I used to feel as a child when my father read me a story. To me, the beginning was always the most fascinating part. The beginning touches something timeless that no events in time can tarnish. Unfortunately, as the story progressed, my interest frittered away, along with my wonder, except for one fairy tale.

In C. S. Lewis's *Last Battle*—the conclusion of *The Chronicles of Narnia* series—there wasn't the usual "and they lived happily ever after." Instead, on the last page, after scores of exhilarating adventures and journeys in all the previous books, C. S. Lewis wrote that now he had come to the beginning of the real story. All the previous chapters of adventures in Narnia had only been the cover and the title page. The real chapter one was about to begin, a story no one on earth had ever read, which would go on forever and ever with each chapter better than the last.

I remember thinking, You mean all that's happened up until now has only been the preface to the real story? All the good

Jesus and heaven are more real than things of earth.

Jesus made a connection between heaven and little children.

stuff was only foreshadowing a greater story! The wonder was back. I was at the beginning again.

Most people wish it were like that in real life. Just as in a story, people labor through chapter after chapter of their lives, and the fascination and wonder they felt as a child fade as the years go by in a succession of events. We grow tired and weary, never able to grasp the dreams that enthralled us at the beginning. The state that we long for is never quite embodied. And so, our interest fritters away.

But for Christians, all the things that stir our interest about eternity will be embodied. We shall behold the Lamb, savor purity, touch truth, and be clothed in righteousness. Like a grand story, it will always be an enchanting beginning—or better yet—the end and the beginning, as God is both *Alpha* and *Omega*, the First and the Last, the Beginning and the End.

You can see the utter impossibility of abstract-thinking adults comprehending heaven. Possibly that's why Jesus made a connection between heaven and little children.

 Get some blank paper and something to draw with, crayons if possible. Try to think like a child again. Draw a picture—if you really get into this assignment, draw a bunch of pictures. Draw those things you will see embodied in heaven, such as truth, purity, and righteousness. Don't make the pictures perfect, draw them with joy as a child would. Plan to share a picture with your study group. You might get inspiration from the following paragraph.

Little wonder flesh and blood cannot inherit heaven. To be at both the beginning and the end, or to wear righteousness like a bright raiment, requires a complete metamorphosis. Like a caterpillar becoming a butterfly or a peach pit becoming a blossoming tree. Our earthly bodies would never be able to contain the joy or express the praise. Our fleshly hearts and minds could never hold it all. Heavenly worship would split the seams and break the human container. We're not talking shedding snakeskins here, we're talking radical transformation. We little caterpillars and peach pits need to go from death to life so that our glorified bodies and hearts are fit for the filling and over-flowing of ecstatic praise. As Jesus declared, "I tell you the truth, no one can see the kingdom of God unless he is born again" (John 3:3).

Praise would be boring if we were able to stop and look at ourselves to see how we were doing, how we were sounding or performing; but such self-consciousness will be foreign in heaven. The crowning glory for us will be in losing ourselves and yet finding ourselves in the *Alpha* and the *Omega*. Pure praise is total preoccupation with God.

Finally, because we will be one with Him, and full of light as He is, our bright, dazzling bodies can't help but be shot through with the glory of God. After all, "glory" is the reflection of God's essential being, whether holiness, justice, compassion, or mercy. Whenever He reveals Himself in any of these qualities on earth or in heaven, we say that He is "glorifying Himself." And in heaven, we, like diamonds, will give off prism-like praise as every facet of our being reflects His *Shekinah* glory. It will be impossible not to praise Him. Daniel 12:3 turns on the light switch when it says, "Those who are wise will shine like the brightness of the heavens, and those who lead many to righteousness, like the stars for ever and ever."

Heaven will shine by the Lamb who is the Lamp. Light will so much be in heaven that "the moon will be abashed, the sun ashamed; for the Lord Almighty will reign on Mount Zion and in Jerusalem, and before its elders, gloriously" (Isaiah 24:23). God's glory and His light go hand in hand. Heaven is a place full of glory, light, and praise.

Who can find words for such worship? What thesaurus has the nouns or adjectives to convey "eating" life like fruit from a tree or "tasting" the Bread of Heaven? I want to lift up my hands and whisper, "Oh, the depth of the riches of the wisdom and knowledge of God! How unsearchable his judgments, and his paths beyond tracing out!... For from him and through him and to him are all things. To him be the glory forever! Amen" (Romans 11:33, 36).

Improve your praise vocabulary by writing a prayer of praise to God. Tell Him why you honor Him. Review the previous paragraphs if you need inspiration.

_____

_____

_____

_____

Pure praise is total preoccupation with God.

Lesson 4

We Will Serve God

I'm speechless. To think that in addition to giving us the blessings of salvation and eternal life, God should reward us with opportunities to serve Him beyond all reasonable proportion. If we think God is generous with His grace to us on earth, wait until we see Him pull out all the stops spreading far and wide His glory in heaven!

That's why I can't get out of my heart or head this thing about crowns. I am awed and inspired by the fact that what I do on earth will have a direct bearing on how I will serve God in heaven. Our present conduct has a bearing on our entrance into heaven and how rich our welcome will be.[13]

Sometimes I feel I'm in the minor leagues, working hard to be ensured a berth somewhere in the major leagues in heaven; because what I do here affects what I get to do there. I'm not talking about earning salvation but about earning rewards. Rewards influence everything from how much heart will go into my eternal worship of God to the kind of job I'll be assigned on the new earth.

Faithfulness is the key.

Faithfulness is the key.

I can see my two macho friends, John and Mike, the ones who hated the idea of doing nothing in heaven, as they stare open-mouthed and wide-eyed after the judgment seat. Now, in heaven, they are sons of God in the fullest sense. What power, what privilege! God has crowned them as proof.

I picture them grabbing each other, jumping up and down, and exclaiming, "Oh boy, now we get to do something! We get to serve!" They rub their hands together, roll up the sleeves on their white robes, and ask, "Okay, Lord, what are our jobs? Just point us in the direction, and we're ready to go!"

 God made us with a passion for work. Most of us even create work for fun—and call them hobbies. Below circle the kinds of "work" you enjoy.

gardening	painting	interior design	hunting
crafts	building things	sewing	landscaping
fishing	reading	cooking	shopping

And, boy, will we do! John and Mike will be on cloud nine, but only for a short time, because they will be busier than they ever were on earth. No idling away eternity strolling streets of gold. No passing time while plucking harps by the glassy sea. We will have jobs to do. I can hardly hold back the tears thinking of my friend Cornelius, who has been bedridden for 15 years, unable to lift a finger to do an ounce of work. I can just see this man now in his glorified body as he tackles all the labor he missed out on those many years on earth. We will serve God through worship and work—exciting work of which we never grow tired.

For me, this will be heaven. I love serving God. And if we've been faithful in earthly service, our responsibility in heaven will increase proportionately. No, I take that back. It won't be increased in proportion. God's too generous for that. Our service will increase completely out of proportion. It doesn't take a rocket scientist to read the formula Jesus gives in His heaven parable in Luke 19:17: "'Well done, my good servant!' his master replied. 'Because you have been trustworthy in a very small matter, take charge of ten cities.'"

Stop and read that again. Ten cities? In exchange for faithfulness in a very small matter? Whoa! When it comes to blessing us, Jesus goes beyond basic math and gets into calculus. Those who are faithful in a few minor things will be put in charge over multitudinous things.

Were you faithful in your marriage or a mission? Even if only in a small way? God is already thinking exponentially, as in His "ten cities" equation. He generously raises your capacity for service to the "nth" degree. The more faithful you are in this life, the more responsibility you will be given in the life to come.

Not Success but Faithfulness

Please note Jesus doesn't say, "Because you've been successful in a very small matter," He says, "Because you've been trustworthy." God is not scrutinizing the success of your marriage or judging the results of your mission. You could have spent 45 years in marriage, 40 of which you were hanging in there by a promise and a prayer. You could have invested 25 years sharing the gospel in the outback of Mozambique with only a handful of converts to show for it. When it comes to the judgment seat, God won't pull out the return-on-investment charts and do a cost-effectiveness analysis on your earthly service. Every Christian is on the same playing field. Success isn't the key.

We will serve God through worship and work.

Faithfulness is. Being bigger and better is not the point. It's being obedient.

 Our society encourages us to measure our "success" in service by "how many did you have." If obedience is the standard, how faithful are you in serving God?

Unfaithful	*Faithful*

The more trustworthy you've been, the greater your service in eternity. Here's where our two buddies will shine!

I have a confession. I'm more like my friends John and Mike than I've admitted. Just spend a few weeks with me and you'll understand. I love rolling up my sleeves down here on earth and pouring myself into serving God. I'm less of a human being, and more of a human doing. Visiting hospitals, advocating issues, shopping for dinner, traveling in ministry, relating in marriage, painting at my easel, writing at my computer, working on radio programs, counseling on the phone, helping with Sunday School, and so on.

I'm also a perfectionist. If a painting is not up to par, I shove it aside. If an article is not up to snuff, I dump it in the trash. If a friendship is injured, I painstakingly repair it. If my marriage is hurting, everything else gets canceled and Ken gets priority. If I feel a speech I give falls flat, I berate myself endlessly, thinking, Why did I say that? ... Why didn't I say this? There have been days when I've thrown up my hands and sighed, "What's the use. I've blown it again!"

A lot of this pressure, because it is self-imposed, is unnecessary. However, some of it is real and needed. God imposes pressure when He knows I've approached service to Him with a lazy, nonchalant attitude.

But in heaven, there will be no failure in service.

No disappointment in doing. We will never struggle with failing to do the task God puts before us, as in a failed marriage or mission. We will never fall short of meeting our responsibilities.

We get to serve and be busier than we ever were on earth.

 What heavenly job would you like to be assigned to do? Use your imagination.

In heaven, there will be no failure in service.

What thought most encourages you about future service in heaven? What thought disturbs you most? Share both thoughts with the Father as you pray to end the lesson.

Lesson 5

We Will Rule the Earth

W e not only get to praise God forever, but we get to reign with Him forever. "To him who overcomes, I will give the right to sit with me on my throne, just as I overcame and sat down with my Father on his throne" (Revelation 3:21). Can you believe it? We will sit with Christ on His throne and reign with Him. We will be given a sphere of authority and oversight of God's eternal kingdom.

We get to reign with Him, plus more.

We are more than kings? Yes, we're sons and heirs. Romans 8:17 elevates us to an incredible position, saying, "Now if we are children, then we are heirs—heirs of God and co-heirs with Christ." Just imagine, we will join Christ in overseeing His and our inheritance. We inherit what our elder Brother inherits. And Psalm 2:8-9 reads like His title deed: "Ask of me, and I will make the nations your inheritance, the ends of the earth your possession. You will rule them with an iron scepter." We're not talking a few acres on the back of the farm. Our sphere of authority will be heaven and earth.

We get to reign over earth with Christ!

I wish I understood the specifics, but God hasn't revealed them all. A hint is whispered in Revelation 20:6 where we are "priests of God and of Christ and will reign with him for a thousand years," and in Isaiah 11:4 where "with righteousness he will judge the needy, with justice he will give decisions for the poor of the earth."

Time and again, the words *inheritance, earth,* and *reign* appear together. Flip through the Old Testament and you see repeated references to God's Anointed personally administering justice, uplifting the oppressed, or ruling with a rod of iron. The particulars may not be laid out, but there's one hint we're supposed to get: We will reign with Christ over the earth.

The possibilities are endless, as well as exhilarating. Maybe our reign on earth will include reforesting the hills of Lebanon,

We get to reign over earth with Christ!

67

helping to judge the wicked, or planting trees along the Amazon. How about clearing the courts of corruption and schooling judges on godly wisdom? How about clearing the slums of Rio de Janeiro or getting rid of nuclear waste? Maybe we'll teach the nations how to worship God, as well as a new definition of peace and how to beat their swords into plowshares. Shall we do a patch job on the ozone layer and make the Blue Danube absolute azure rather than mud-brown? Cut government fat, get rid of red tape, and show everyone that a theocracy is the only rule in town?

One thing's for sure. There will be no homeless men and women! No orphanages or mental hospitals. No abortion clinics. And no nursing homes for old people.

In the midst of it all, the glittering capital city of heaven, the New Jerusalem, will be set like a gleaming pearl. Kings and princes will pour into the Holy City from the far corners of the earth to pay homage. The image blows my mind, but it's laid out as clear as crystal glass in Revelation 21.

I realize this raises more questions than answers. Like, who are all these people who have to be ruled with a rod of iron? After the return to earth of the Lord Jesus and His saints, what are all those other folks still doing on earth? Some scholars say that after the dead in Christ are raised at His return to earth, we will reign with Him over the people of this planet for a thousand years. At the close of this period, the devil will incite one last rebellion, which will kick off Armageddon. God's armies will win, the devil will lose, wicked people will be resurrected, the Book of Life will be opened, and the Day of Judgment will have come. After the final destruction of that old serpent and his wicked hordes, earth will be consumed in fire, cleansed, and made fit for eternal habitation. Got that?

Other scholars assert that when the Lord Jesus comes to earth as King of kings, time will end after an immediate Armageddon, the defeat of Satan, the judgment of the dead, and a fiery holocaust that incinerates all of the earth and space beyond. When the smokes clears, the Lord and His saints will set up the eternal kingdom in the new heavens and new earth.

How the earth, whether new or old, fits into God's heavenly scheme of things, I can't say for certain. I tend toward the view that we shall reign with Christ on this earth for a thousand years, this period being a kind of vestibule to heaven. But all I really need to know is "we are looking forward to a new heaven and a new earth, the home of righteousness" (2 Peter 3:13). Heaven will feel like home. I will be a co-heir with Christ. I will

Heaven will feel like home.

help rule in the new heavens and the new earth. And I will be busier and happier in service than I ever dreamed possible.

And you will be too.

Ruling Angels and Demons

 Read 1 Corinthians 6:2-3, which appears in the margin. The verse states that we will be judges. Underline the phrases that describe who and what we will judge.

Angels will be subject to us in eternity. We will reign with Jesus. If He has been given authority over all the heavenly hosts, then we will reign over angels too. Will we govern a few legions or many? What shall we command them to do? How will they aid us on earth to help carry out the kingdom rule? I can't say, but it's thrilling to imagine. I'm sure glad I'll have a glorified mind to handle it. Strategic leadership will be a cinch for us. We'll be able to rally angelic legions, as well as lead the way in doing God's work in heaven and on earth.

One more thing. When it comes to fallen angels—demons— we will judge them. If 1 Corinthians 6:2-3 didn't spell it out in black and white, I'd laugh at the improbability of it all.

Incredible!

This short but powerful Scripture is another one of those exponential statements that smack of an almost unbelievable increase in our capacity to serve, as well as our responsibility in ruling. Once again, God will blow out all formulas on proportions and put us in charge of judging fallen angels. I cringe at the idea. On earth I'm having a tough enough time deciding who's right in a friendly spat, who ought to get the last piece of pie or whether or not justice was served in a local court case.

Me? Judging angels? Again, I breathe a sigh of relief to know that I will have all of God's wisdom at my disposal; otherwise, the job would send me cowering. It's just another way we will rule with Christ in heaven.

Frankly, the idea intrigues me. I can't wait to nail a couple of evil spirits. On earth, I have been so harassed by troublesome demons of temptation or evil forces who keep trying to trip me up. I'm not saying "the devil made me do it" on earth; I take full responsibility for my choices and actions. But demons sure haven't helped. I could easily throw the book at them!

Then there are the more heinous powers and principalities of darkness who have incited wicked men to wreck havoc. These are the gruesome demons under Satan who for centuries have

Do you not know that the saints will judge the world? And if you are to judge the world, are you not competent to judge trivial cases? Do you not know that we will judge angels? How much more the things of this life!
—1 Corinthians 6:2-3

pushed evil men further into rebellion, murder, torture, and grisly massacres. I especially detest those forces of evil behind the crucifixion of God's own Son, who urged those drunken soldiers to slap and spit on the Second Person of the Trinity.

 You or your loved ones may have experienced injustice during your earthly journey. You will one day be able to share in bringing justice to the demonic spirits behind those acts. Does this promise comfort you when you recall past injustice or suffering? ❏ Yes ❏ No ❏ Somewhat

How does it enhance your understanding of God's justice?

_____

_____

I can hardly wait for that glorious day when Satan and his legions will be punished and eternally tormented for their procuring the fall of mankind. One day we shall have the pleasure of demonstrating "perfect hatred,"against the rulers, powers, and principalities of darkness.

Satan and his legions will be punished for their procuring the fall of mankind.

More Real Than We Can Imagine
You know what thrills me most about reigning with Christ on earth? It's concrete. Heaven is not some never-neverland of thin, ghostly shapes and clouds. It's not a place where you can poke your finger through people only to discover that they are spacy spirit beings you can't really hug or hold. No way!

Just writing the last few pages has invigorated my excitement over how like the Rock of Gibraltar heaven is. We shall touch and taste, rule and reign, move and run, laugh and never cry.

Maybe years ago I assumed heaven was a misty, nebulous home for angels and—gulp!—humans, but not now. I get tickled thinking about how rock-solid real heaven is, and how much of a home—much more so than earth—it will be.

A real reign on a real earth.

And our Savior, our King of kings, leading the way.

 Review this unit briefly by looking at your responses to the learning activities. From your work this week, write in the margin three actions you can take to grow your love for the Father and your passion to honor Him.

Unit 4

Why Don't We Fit on Earth?

As Christians, you and I are not made for this world. Well, in one sense we are. Our hands, feet, eyes, and ears equip us for physical experiences on this planet made of water and dirt. Our ears process noise, our eyes register sights, our noses detect odors, and our stomachs digest food. But we are also spirit. Someone once said, "Through faith we understand that we are not physical beings having a spiritual experience, but spiritual beings having a physical experience."

I like earth. But my heart pumps for heaven.

Calabasas, California, is nice, but it pales in the light of the heavenly realms. Home is pretty good here, but my homing instincts often have me shade my eyes and scan "a land that stretches afar." I have a glorious homesickness for heaven, a penetrating and piercing ache. I'm a stranger in a strange land, a displaced person with a fervent and passionate pain that is, oh, so satisfying. The groans are a blessing. What a sweetness to feel homesick for heaven for "a longing fulfilled is sweet to the soul" (Proverbs 13:19).

The good things in this world are pleasant enough, but would we really wish for it to go on as it is? I don't think so. The nice things in this life are merely omens of even greater, more glorious things yet to come. God would not have us mistake this world for a permanent dwelling. C. S. Lewis said something about not mistaking pleasant inns for home on our journey to heaven. I'm with him. It's a good life, but I am looking forward to going home.

I miss my home.

I miss God.

This week you will explore what being a stranger in a strange land means. This world cannot truly be home for those who are bound for heaven. Learn more about your *real* home!

Our citizenship is in heaven. And we eagerly await a Savior from there, the Lord Jesus Christ, who, by the power that enables him to bring everything under his control, will transform our lowly bodies so that they will be like his glorious body. —Philippians 3:20-21

What You'll Learn in This Unit

Unit Scripture

71

Lesson 1

We Feel Displaced

ey, lady, your suitcase is over there!" a baggage handler yelled.

"Get that cart out of the way, would ya!"

"Taxi! Hey, stop—I said, 'Taxi!' " someone hollered outside.

It was mayhem. My friend was steering me in my wheelchair through thick crowds and piles of suitcases in the baggage claim area of the Los Angeles airport.

While I waited in the midst of pandemonium, I did what I always do. I sat still. Very still.

It's a fact of life. Because I'm paralyzed from the shoulders down, a large part of me never moves. I have instant stillness. Even when rushing, I stay put in my wheelchair. I could be scurrying through a jam-packed schedule, doing this and that, but a big part of me—due to my paralysis—is always quiet.

 Circle the common phrase in all three Scriptures in the margin.

You may not have to be still physically, as I do, but we all need to be still on the inside before God. That's the lesson this chair keeps teaching me, and that's why, if you had seen me in that busy airport, you would have noticed a satisfied smile. In an earlier time I would have felt trapped, useless, and resentful that I could not grab my own suitcase, elbow the guy who butted in line, or hail my own taxi. But faith, honed and sharpened from years in my wheelchair, has changed that. So I sat there thanking God for built-in quiet and stillness before Him.

God has used my chair to change me. Do you have a "wheelchair" in your life? If so, are you cursing your predicament or praising God for the stillness? Take a moment to thank the loving Father who turns our most painful trial to our greatest blessing.

I also thought about heaven. With eyes of faith I looked beyond the sight of bumper-to-bumper traffic, the smell of sweat, cigarettes, exhaust fumes, and the sounds of my harried co-travelers, and began humming quietly...

This world is not my home, I'm just a passing through,
My treasures are laid up somewhere beyond the blue;
The angels beckon me from heaven's open door,
And I can't feel at home in this world anymore.[14]

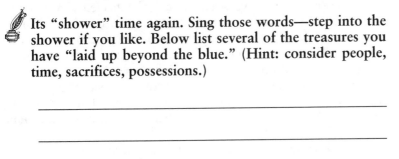 Its "shower" time again. Sing those words—step into the shower if you like. Below list several of the treasures you have "laid up beyond the blue." (Hint: consider people, time, sacrifices, possessions.)

_____

_____

_____

I hum that haunting tune in other places besides the Los Angeles airport. Sometimes I get that "can't feel at home" sensation ambling down the aisles of K-Mart, watching women grab blue-light specials. Sometimes it happens sitting with Ken watching Monday Night Football's fourth instant replay of a third-down conversion. I definitely feel "this world is not my home" as I sit on the Ventura-Freeway-turned-parking-lot.

Don't think I'm strange. Christians have felt the same for centuries. Malcolm Muggeridge, a British journalist who spent most of his years battling Christianity, finally succumbed to Christ in his seventies. The intellectual world had always been home to him, but now, in the hallowed halls of university life, he found himself saying,

I had a sense, sometimes enormously vivid, that I was a stranger in a strange land; a visitor, not a native ... a displaced person. ... The feeling, I was surprised to find, gave me a great sense of satisfaction, almost of ecstasy. ... Days or weeks or months might pass. Would it ever return—the lostness? I strain my ears to hear it, like distant music; my eyes to see it, a very bright light very far away. Has it gone forever? And then—ah! the relief. Like slipping away from a sleeping embrace, silently shutting a door behind one, tiptoeing off in the grey light of dawn— a stranger again. The only ultimate disaster that can befall us, I have come to realize, is to feel ourselves to be at home here on earth. As long as we are aliens, we cannot forget our true homeland.[15]

The only ultimate disaster that can befall us is to feel ourselves to be at home here on earth.

 Wow! Don't let that one slip away from you. In the margin write in your own words why feeling at home here is a disaster.

His words could have been mine as I wheeled through the Thousand Oaks Mall yesterday. I was a stranger in a strange land between the video game parlor on the second floor and the first floor movie complex running the latest Arnold Schwarzenegger film. Actually, I felt like a blessed stranger. A displaced, but satisfied person. Everyone seemed absorbed by the fashion show in the center courtyard, but I found myself thinking, *Does anyone else realize that there's more to life than the new fall designs?*

In the learning activity above, I asked why feeling at home here is a disaster. Many answers apply, but the key danger is forgetting our true home is heaven, not earth.

That's what blessed strangers and satisfied displaced persons feel. They see that heaven is home. It's where we belong. "We all have a homing instinct, a 'home detector,' and it doesn't ring for earth," says Peter Kreeft.[16]

I did not feel at home in that mall. I saw its world as trite and commonplace. I didn't view the people as banal or boring; if anything, my heart went out to the kids hanging around the video parlor and the ladies watching the fashion show. The troubling part was the "world" in which they were engrossed.

I couldn't help but see something past this world, not unlike the moment of faith I experienced in the Los Angeles airport. How so? Faith is double-sided. It not only verifies heaven as real, but it also makes us look differently at visible things on earth. Through faith's eyes, heaven becomes a rock-solid home. The concrete world in which we live becomes drained of substance and importance. When we look at life through eyes of faith, things around us no longer possess the glow of excitement.

If I forget you, O Jerusalem, may my right hand forget its skill.
—Psalm 137:5

 The writer of Psalm 137 was in exile away from Jerusalem. You see by the words in the margin how passionately he wanted to remember his home. Paraphrase the psalmist's words to declare your passion for heaven.

I long for my heavenly home because _____

_____

I'm not encouraging you to throw away your talents by praying, "Lord, take away my skill." But I challenge you to pile everything else up beside what God has in store for those that love Him—then choose the better pile.

Because faith makes invisible things real, and visible things unreal, earthly dissatisfaction becomes the road to heavenly satisfaction. Heaven supplants the earth as home.

 Read Philippians 3:18-19 in the margin. Ask God to take your focus off earthly things. Talk to Him about your journey as a "stranger in a strange land."

Many live as enemies of the cross of Christ. Their destiny is destruction... Their mind is on earthly things.
—*Philippians 3:18-19*

Lesson 2

We Identify with Strangers

Faith causes us to identify with strangers. The more home-like heaven becomes, the more you feel like an alien and stranger on earth. "Our citizenship is in heaven" (Philippians 3:20). I'm not talking spiritual snobbery here, and I have no beef against Lexus cars or knits by St. John's. It's simply a matter of focus: "For where your treasure is, there your heart will be also" (Matthew 6:21).

Even if you're not in the habit of memorizing Scripture, may I suggest a couple of great verses? Copy Philippians 3:20-21 on a note card and carry it with you. Review it several times a day. Memorize part of the passage at a time.

Please don't think I drive a clunker, wear my sister's hand-me-downs, hate the mall, and never turn on a television. I like nice stuff. There's nothing trite, banal, or boring about these pleasures. This feeling of being an alien or stranger on earth has more to do with the song I told you about in the introduction. The haunting echo. The writer of Hebrews 11:14-16 definitely had me in mind when he said, "People who say such things show that they are looking for a country of their own. If they had been thinking of the country they had left, they would have had opportunity to return. Instead, they were longing for a better country—a heavenly one."

Our citizenship is in heaven. And we eagerly await a Savior from there, the Lord Jesus Christ, who, by the power that enables him to bring everything under his control, will transform our lowly bodies so that they will be like his glorious body.
—*Philippians 3:20-21*

 Do a bit of spiritual brainstorming. The verse said they looked for a better country. In the margin write as many ways as you can think of that heaven is a better country. Be prepared to share your list with your group this week.

I'm a little like a refugee who is longing for my better country called heaven. My heart is in quasi-exile. In fact, 1 Kings 11:14-22 is just a brief story, but it's "me" all over. It seems that Hadad, an adversary of Solomon, had fled for safety to Egypt with some of his father's family. There he found great favor with Pharaoh, married into the king's family, and reared his son in the royal palace. But when he heard that David was dead, "Hadad said to Pharaoh, 'Let me go, that I may return to my own country.'"

"'What have you lacked here that you want to go back to your own country?' Pharaoh asked."

"'Nothing,' Hadad replied, 'but do let me go!'"

That's the part I identify with. Earth may be rich with past memories and present moments as it was with Hadad, but I'm hot on his heels: "Let me go, that I may return to my own country." It is always the exiles who remember home. The Israelites, captive in a foreign land, remembered their true country when they mourned in Psalm 137:1: "By the rivers of Babylon we sat and wept when we remembered Zion." Like Hadad, like the Israelites, I carry in my exiled heart a hunger for my heavenly country, my soul's true home.

A person who feels at home "fits" with his environment, like a fish in water, a bird in the sky, or a worm in the dirt. But we don't "fit" here. It's not our environment. There is no harmony, no "rightness," with our surroundings. Remember my experiences in the Los Angeles airport and the Thousand Oaks Mall? It wasn't as though the hustle and bustle of that world offended me; it's just that it didn't jibe, it didn't resonate with the peace and stillness in my heart, a peace that echoed, "You don't belong here."[17]

Feeling like an exile is simply feeling a fact.

Homesick for Heaven
We pilgrims walk the tightrope between earth and heaven, feeling trapped in time, yet with eternity beating in our hearts. Our unsatisfied sense of exile is not to be solved or fixed while here on earth. Our pain and longings make sure we will never be content, but that's good: it is to our benefit that we do not grow comfortable in a world destined for decay.

I carry in my exiled heart a hunger for my heavenly country, my soul's true home.

And so we squirm and writhe, knowing we don't quite fit; "we groan, longing to be clothed with our heavenly dwelling." But, oh, what a blessing are those groans! What a sweetness to feel homesick for heaven! What a glorious longing fills my heart to overflowing! In heaven we will be where we belong.

 Have you ever been really homesick? If so, remember that experience. Where were you, when, and why? How did you feel? Be prepared to share the experience in your group this week. Make notes in the space below.

_____

_____

Wait a minute, Joni, perhaps you are thinking. *I'm not homesick for heaven. I rarely groan and long to be there ... I want to, but I don't know where to begin. It's not like I'm absorbed by the things of earth; it's just heaven doesn't feel like my home yet.*

If this is you, don't panic. If, for you, heaven is still a glass house on some golden street rather than a warm and loving home, then hang in there. If you find it difficult to muster up longing for celestial mansions, if you aren't into this pilgrim thing, then perhaps we need to take the focus off heaven as a place. It's more than that ... much, much more.

 When you recall a time of homesickness, what percentage of your homesickness was for a place and what percentage was for one or more persons?

____ % for a place
____ % for a person(s)

I sometimes feel nostalgic about a place, but I usually find I miss people more than places. Think of those times in groups or situations where you felt like you truly belonged. Why did you sense that you "fit"? Ultimately our longing for heaven is a longing for God, our true lover whom earthly lovers can only imitate. Home is where love is.

Until we are there, doing what God purposed for us from the beginning, we will be the caterpillar writhing to be free of the cocoon, to breathe celestial air. We will feel very much like Moses cocooned away in the back side of a desert who cried,

Perhaps we need to take the focus off heaven as a place.

"I have become an alien in a foreign land" (Exodus 2:22). And just as Moses was becoming, in the desert, the leader he would eventually be, we are pilgrims becoming, in the here and now, who we shall be in the hereafter.

So, on we pilgrims tread through this world of time and death, forever seeking the Son. We don't go backward but, "Forgetting what is behind and straining toward what is ahead, [we] press on toward the goal to win the prize for which God has called [us] heavenward in Christ Jesus" (Philippians 3:13-14).

General humanity refuses to go in this direction. In an anxious search to fit, people take the world's sextant and try to locate their present position using all the wrong coordinates: memories of childhood, an old romance, carefree days, songs, power, religion, wealth, or Woodstock. But humanity keeps failing to recognize that it is "made in the image of God." Only believers who understand that the coordinates converge in eternity can sing, "This world is not my home."

Philippians 3:21 says Jesus will transform us to be like Him. Talk with Him about the ways you desire to be transformed. Consider your relationships to material things, others, your work, your worship, and your body.

Lesson 3

We Are Shielded by Sin

A thick shield still stands between God and us.

A thick shield still stands between God and us. We cannot see what our heart longs to because as 1 Timothy 6:16 says, "[God] lives in unapproachable light, whom no one has seen nor can see." When Moses pressed hard upon God to see His face, he would have been glad to use thick glass coated with UV block and grab a quick peek at God through his fingers. But, no. Moses was only permitted to glimpse the backside of God's glory, for the Lord warned, "My face must not be seen" (Exodus 33:23). God didn't hide His face because there was nothing for Moses to see; He knew His light would kill. No man can see God and live. The Lord's glorious radiance would have snuffed Moses out in a nanosecond.

Even when Isaiah "saw" the Lord high and exalted on a throne, he did not behold God's face. He only glimpsed the periphery of the radiance of God. The sight threw Isaiah so deeply into despair over his sin that he cried, "Woe to me! ... I am ruined! For I am a man of unclean lips" (Isaiah 6:5).

Sin is the problem. Sin is more than a thick shield between God and us. Acknowledging our stockpile of iniquities won't make it go away. No amount of confessing will help us see God. That's backward. We don't have a clue as to the heinous nature of our sin until first we glimpse God's radiance, and then the words come tumbling out, "Woe is me!" The closer the apostle Paul got to God, the more he cried, "I am the chief of sinners." I used to think Paul was pompous, grandstanding, but not any more. It's the cry of the saint sensitized to sin.

 The way we view sin indicates our sensitivity to it. All of the following definitions describe sin. From the list select the five ways you most commonly think of sin.

___ missing the mark	___ unbelief
___ offending God	___ rebellion
___ breaking the law	___ pride
___ willful disobedience	___ spiritual adultery
___ seeking to take God's place	___ guilt
___ other _____	

None of these phrases adequately describes the mystery and tragedy of human sin. We long to see God, whether we know it or not, to see our sins exposed and to be cleansed by God Himself. Just as guilt will cause a child to hide in shame from her daddy's face, our deepest desire is to be clean, free, and transparent before the Father. It won't happen until we see His face.[18]

This is a living paradox. We desire to see the face of God, but we cringe at seeing the face of God. We are cleansed from our sin, but we're still unclean. We're justified before God, but we've got miles of sanctification to go before we sleep. We're in the household of God but not home yet. Our eyes are opened, but we can only see through a glass darkly. It's frustrating!

 Do you identify with the paradox of faith? Describe a time when you—

longed to see the face of God _____

_____

Our deepest desire is to be clean, free, and transparent before the Father.

cringed at the thought of seeing the face of God. _____

_____

Our sin problem is partly why it's so difficult to muster strong feelings about heaven. You and I going to heaven for a wedding? Our wedding? "His bride has made herself ready. Fine linen, bright and clean" (Revelation 19:7-8). "Fine linen" stands for the righteous acts of the saints. Righteous acts! We glance down and see stains and smudges all over our wedding gown, which, by the way, is tearing at the seams and missing a few pearls and fasteners. Little wonder we cower at seeing our Bridegroom.

True, we presently see stains and smudges all over us, and we cower, thinking, He'll never see anything lovely in me. But still, we ache to see Him. And so we live in hope. God will find us and He will not always remain beyond our sight.

 Which of the following best describes what you see when you look at yourself?

❑ fine linen
❑ smears and smudges

What does your response tell you about how you see yourself?

_____

_____

What does your response tell you about how you see the Bridegroom?

_____

_____

Our Bridegroom desires that I long and look for Him "while we wait for the blessed hope." And "everyone who has this hope in him purifies himself, just as he is pure" (1 John 3:3). It's called "being prepared," all you saints in your torn bridal garments, and "it teaches us to say 'No' to ungodliness and worldly passions, and to live self-controlled, upright and godly lives in this present age, while we wait for the blessed hope—the glorious appearing of our great God and Savior, Jesus Christ, who gave himself for us to redeem us from all wickedness and to purify for himself a people that are his very own, eager to do what is good" (Titus 2:12-14).

One day He will come for us and look into our eyes. We will hold His gaze. And all the stains and smears of sin will be purified out of us just by one searching of those eyes. It will be more than we dreamed of, more than we longed for.

All That Are in Hell, Choose It

It's unthinkable to talk about heaven without at least mentioning hell. Please note I didn't refer to it as "heaven's counterpart." Heaven has no counterpart. It has no opposite. Just as Satan is not God's opposite (for the devil is merely a created being—and a fallen one, at that!), neither does heaven have an opposite. In the vastness of God's infinite, as well as cleansed and purified universe, hell may end up being only a speck. A trash heap. A garbage dump.

Outside of Jerusalem, the holy city, there was a junkyard where the Jews took their garbage to burn. In earlier times pagan tribes, and wayward Jews themselves, had used this area called GeHinnom for performing rituals and sacrifices. God's people thought it only a place fit to set fire to their waste. They ended up calling it Gehenna, the biblical term for hell.

Peter Kreeft describes the rationale for hell this way:

> *God makes no garbage, but we do; and a good cosmos must eventually purify itself of spiritual garbage like egotism, hate, greed, cowardice, or lust. ... We can even rejoice that hell exists, for we should want our spiritual garbage burned away, if we do not identify ourselves with that garbage. If we do, we are burned eternally. ... God cannot allow that garbage into heaven; and if we do not want to throw it away, if we clutch our garbage so close that we become garbage, there is only one place for us.*[19]

Hell will not pollute the purified universe, nor will it be a festering boil in the side of the new heavens, an ugly sore spot that forever seeps and demands somebody's attention. It may well be too small for that. I don't mean hell will be smaller than heaven in terms of population statistics, but in terms of its importance in the new heavens and new earth. Nobody pays much attention to smoldering junk heaps.

Jesus' teaching about hell with its wormwood and gall is meant to strike terror in our hearts, warning us that if heaven is

Heaven has no counterpart. It has no opposite.

better than we could dream, so hell will be worse than we can imagine.

Hell warns us to seek heaven. It is its own best deterrent.

 Pretend that you are on a debate team. Your subject is this statement: *The existence of hell proves that God is mean and vindictive.* **You are to argue against the statement. In the margin outline your argument using the paragraphs above along with any other thoughts or resources.**

Does it seem unfair? Does it seem cruel that unbelievers "will be thrown outside, into the darkness, where there will be weeping and gnashing of teeth" (Matthew 8:12)? Our human sense of justice may think so, but remember, God owes this utterly rebellious planet absolutely nothing.

 According to the verse in the margin, what was our condition before Christ came into our lives?

Were it not for God's quickening grace, we would all remain dead in our trespasses. Were it not for His grace, this planet would have ripped itself apart at the seams long ago in hatred and violence. That the human race has survived this long is a demonstration of God's compassion. The question, "How could God let so many people go to hell?" should be "How could God be so generous and save as many as He does?"

Human fairness is not the point; the justice of God is. If there's no judgment and subsequent hell, then it makes more sense to eat, drink, and be merry for tomorrow we die and ... period. Nothingness. It's all over. But there is a hell as well as a judgment. "I saw the dead, great and small, standing before the throne, and books were opened. Another book was opened, which is the book of life. The dead were judged according to what they had done ... If anyone's name was not found written in the book of life, he was thrown into the lake of fire" (Revelation 20:12, 15).

Revelation 20:15 makes my hair stand on end. Apocalyptic verses about signs of the times, earthquakes, floods, and pestilence don't do it. Not even word pictures about snarling beasts and ten-horned creatures or the heavens rolling up as a scroll and the mountains fleeing into the ocean. The worst verse is the one about dead people being judged. Some of those dead will be persons I know and many I love.

Because of his great love for us, God, who is rich in mercy, made us alive with Christ even when we were dead in transgressions—it is by grace you have been saved.
—Ephesians 2:4-5

When I pray, "Come quickly, Lord Jesus," I utter that word "quickly" with caution. Do I really want Jesus to return soon? Yes!

And no.

 In the margin list the names of at least five people for whom you are concerned because they do not know Jesus. Pray for them and for yourself. Pray for the opportunity and courage to share a testimony with them.

Lesson 4
We Cannot Transcend Time

As spiritual beings, you and I are not made for this world because the earth is temporal. There is something in us that is definitely not temporal. That's why we squirm and groan against the confines of time. The clock, for us, is an adversary. Every heavenly moment—whether it be gazing into the soft eyes and gentle smile of the one we love or relishing the ecstasy of some glorious pleasure—every moment like this we embrace so we might keep time at bay. But we can't. We would like to call these moments timeless, but they're not. Time snatches them from our grasp.

Time is where the tension really kicks in. In one sense, as Sheldon Vanauken writes, "Time is our natural environment. We live in time as we live in the air we breathe. And we love the air. ... How strange that we cannot love time. It spoils our loveliest moments. ... We wished to know, to savor, to sink in— into the heart of the experience—to possess it wholly. But there was never enough time."[20] I can't explain the tension any better than that. Time is our natural environment, yet time is not our natural environment.

 Where on the continuum below do your feelings about time fall? I see time as...

An enemy
stealing my moments,
days, and years.

A friend,
ushering me closer
to heaven.

People who don't believe in God consider time an adversary.

It's not just Christians who kick against the traces of time. People who don't believe in God consider time an adversary. For them, the ticking of the second hand sounds like the stalking of an enemy. Each minute moves them toward death. And everyone, whether rich or poor, tries to grab the hour hand to shove it backward. "Slow down and live" is a slogan on everything from highway signs to health books. But we can't slow down time. Wrinkle cream won't do it. Pumping your brain and brawn with Vitamins E and A won't do it. And freezing your body in an iced hydrogen chamber won't stop time either. It's the honest person who would agree with C. S. Lewis when he says, "Time itself is one more name for death."[21]

All of humanity senses this, for, "He has also set eternity in the hearts of men; yet they cannot fathom what God has done from beginning to end" (Ecclesiastes 3:11). Yes, people in general just can't fathom God, let alone this thing about a timeless eternity. They don't know what to do with it except to buy Shirley MacLaine's latest New Age best-seller or apply more Oil of Olay. Their only real recourse against the onslaught of time is their memories.

Longing for Another Time

I know what it's like to grab hold of memories, like bricks, and build a dike against time. When I was first paralyzed in 1967—and still new to this eternity thing as a young Christian—heaven was in no way my home. I was less interested in looking forward to a glorified body and more interested in turning back the clock to days when my body worked. Time was an enemy. It kept putting more distance between the past on my feet and the present in my wheelchair. The only way I could slow down the weeks and months was to dive into my memories.

I couldn't do much but listen to the radio or records. Folk music still lingered in the late sixties, and I found refuge in Joni Mitchell's restless songs about the past. Her music evoked a more powerful and fundamental nostalgia than pining for a lost love or a trouble-free yesterday. Listen to the ache and the haunting longing in her song called "Woodstock":

> *We are stardust, we are golden,*
> *Caught up in the devil's bargain,*
> *And we've got to get ourselves*
> *Back to the Garden.*
> *We've got to get ourselves*
> *Back to a semblance of a God.*[22]

Joni Mitchell and thousands like her are looking for something incalculably precious they've lost, something they've got to get back to. They may mistake it for the nostalgia of the sixties or the fifties, a yesterday when one's troubles seemed so far away, but it's much more than that. It's a nostalgia not for the innocence of youth, but for the innocence of humanity. "We've got to get ourselves back to the Garden," a lost world groans. It's Eden where we lost not just our youth, but our identity.

 If you had an opportunity to sit down with Joni Mitchell, what would you want to tell her about her search for a lost identity? about the lost garden? about getting back to God?

We may not realize it, but all of humanity is exiled from the bliss of the intimate presence of God, "walking in the Garden in the cool of the evening." But being "dead in our trespasses," humanity doesn't realize this is what it longs for. Most people don't understand that to walk with God is to feel at home.

What's funny is I'm convinced even if people could reach back into the Garden, if Joni Mitchell could go back to the moment of the creation of the world, it wouldn't be enough.

If we could return to the garden, to innocence, what would we be missing? Write in the margin.

I asked you a difficult one. A theologian might say that we "gained more in Christ than we lost in Adam." If we only went back to our original state, we would be coheirs with Adam and be innocent again; but God has made us coheirs with Christ and this means going beyond innocence and gaining the righteousness of Christ. We wouldn't know the experience of being redeemed and forgiven, of being Christ's bride.

If Joni Mitchell could get back to Eden, she'd stand there in the middle of a perfect environment and feel perfectly ill at ease, not realizing satisfaction could only be found by taking one more step off the edge of time itself and into the mind of God. Our nostalgia for Eden is not just for another time, but another kind of time. Those who do not believe still feel the tug. Even those who do not hope for heaven still wrestle with this vexing enigma of "eternity" set in their hearts.

Most people have it backward.

Unlike those who don't believe in God, our road is not back to the Garden of Eden, but forward. One should never look

Most people don't understand that to walk with God is to feel at home.

over one's shoulder on the road of hope. In Genesis, God sent the seraphim with the flaming sword to bar Adam and Eve from returning to Eden once they had fallen. "The road to God lies ahead, 'east of Eden,' through the world of time and history, struggle and suffering and death. Ejected from Eden's eastern gate, we travel through and around the world, from west to east, forever seeking the rising sun (the Rising Son!) and find Him standing at the western gate ... saying, 'I am the door.'"[23]

We find Him standing at the western gate saying, "I am the door."

Our Place in Time

Joni Mitchell won't make it back to the garden. She would do better to sing of God's Son in her quest for identity, for another time. Jesus is the only One who was ever comfortable with His identity, as well as comfortable in or out of time.

One second Jesus could be conversing with friends on the road to Emmaus, the next He could bypass the hours required to travel to Jerusalem and appear there in no time flat. He could materialize one morning on a beach, then start a fire and whip up breakfast for His friends. One minute He could eat a fish, the next pass through a wall. Stone walls and unopened doors in the upper room presented no barriers. Time, space, and therefore distance were a cinch. His ability to move in and out of various dimensions clues us in to where time fits in heaven. I don't think heaven will destroy time so much as swallow it up.

In eternity everything is just a beginning. No borders. No limits. Our pilgrimage to heaven is not a journey toward the end of time, but to another kind of time. And time travelers we shall be until we arrive ... at the beginning.

 Review the last three paragraphs of this lesson. In the margin write one idea or statement that thrills you about heaven.

Lesson 5

We Long for Unseen Realities

This dusty little planet keeps spinning through time and space, not realizing that all the while it is swimming in the ocean of eternity and surrounded by a host of unseen divine realities. But we realize it because as pilgrims "we live by faith, not by sight" (2 Corinthians 5:7). By faith we live on a different plane, in another dimension, at a higher level than the earthly one. By faith the rock-solid world becomes drained of substance and importance. We see a heavenly meaning behind everything.

🕊 **What do eyes of faith see when they view a mountain range, a cherry tree, the ocean, or the human body? After you've given it some thought, read on.**

People who lack faith look at the front range of the Rocky Mountains and assume, in a mechanistic way, that a tectonic plate pushed this way and that, causing a quake and a shifting in the earth's crust then—*voilà*—there appeared Pikes Peak. But pilgrims heading for heaven realize that "by him all things were created: things in heaven and on earth, visible and invisible, whether thrones or powers or rulers or authorities; all things were created by him and for him" (Colossians 1:16). He has created invisible things that are just as real—no, more real—than the Rocky Mountains. No wonder we praise our Creator!

People who lack faith look at a beautiful cherry tree, shrug their shoulders and suppose a seed fell, rain poured, roots sprouted, a sapling grew, and soon it shall be someone's firewood. God just wound nature up like a clock to let it ticktock on its way. People with heaven-inspired faith, look at the same tree and marvel that literally "in him all things hold together" (Colossians 1:17). That means right now. This instant. Even buds, bark, and branches. Elizabeth Barrett Browning wrote:

> *Earth's crammed with heaven,*
> *And every common bush afire with God;*
> *But only he who sees takes off his shoes,*
> *The rest sit 'round it and pluck blackberries.*

Those with an earthly perspective assume that the waves of the sea are made up of plain old H_2O, but those with a heavenly point of view believe that every proton on the Periodic Table of the Elements is held together by God, for He is "sustaining all things by his powerful word" (Hebrews 1:3). Let that fact sink in. If God were to withdraw His command, the mountains, oceans, and trees wouldn't collapse into chaos, they would go poof and disappear! God's creation isn't static and inert, it's dynamic and actually in the process of being sustained this instant by His powerful word.

God's creation is being sustained this instant by His powerful word.

*Faith imparts heavenly
purpose to everything
around us.*

When it comes to the marvel of the human body, those who
have no faith claim we've risen out of slime to the status of
homo erectus and assume that humans draw breath under their
own power. But pilgrims with a heart for heaven know differently, "for in him we live and move and have our being" (Acts
17:28). In heaven we will be more the man or the woman than
what our gender only whispered of on earth.

The faith of which I've been speaking imparts heavenly purpose to everything around us. Every Tuesday, Wednesday, and
Thursday morning my artist friend, Patti, helps get me out of
bed. Before I get in the van and she sends me off to work, we
pause at the the opened garage door and take a few moments
to observe the day. We look at Mr. Aquilevech's white pine
trees across the street. We admire the way Mrs. Hollander's
shrubs are starting to turn color from a silvery green to gold.

Commenting on a hibiscus bloom, Patti notes, "God
dreamed up that color! Perhaps just for the sheer fun of it."
Pilgrims see His delight in giving us pleasure. Heavenly
sojourners see God in everything. With such faith it is truly
possible to please Him (Hebrews 11:6).

 To what degree do you look at your world as "held
together" by and "afire with" God? To answer that question, complete the following inventory. Circle your
response to each statement, where 1 = always, 2 = usually,
3 = sometimes, and 4 = seldom or never.

When I see "natural" beauty, I think, "God made that."	1 2 3 4
When I encounter evil, my first thought is, "How that must hurt the heart of God."	1 2 3 4
When I experience goodness, I see God at work.	1 2 3 4
When bad things happen, I expect God to bring good from the ashes.	1 2 3 4

 You probably circled 2, 3, or 4 most of the time. If you
could answer "always" to each statement, what difference
do you realistically think it would make in your life?

Madame Guyon, a seventeenth-century Christian noble-
woman, wrote the following words from a French dungeon,

having no hibiscus, cedar tree, sweet green earth, or soft blue heaven to cheer her on:

> *[The heaven-minded Christian] walks by a simple and pure faith, ... and when this sojourner looks out of his own eyes, he sees things as though he were looking through the eyes of God. He sees his own life, he sees his surrounding circumstances, he sees other believers, he sees friends and enemies, he sees principalities and powers, he sees the whole course of the pageantry of history itself through the eyes of God ... and is content.*[24]

Too Heavenly Minded?

Don't think such heavenly mindedness makes us pilgrims no earthly good. Sojourners who think the most of the next world are usually those who are doing the highest good in this one. The person whose mind is only on earthly things does little good on earth. C. S. Lewis expands on this, saying, "Aim at heaven and you get earth thrown in. Aim at earth and you get neither."[25]

 Do you believe the statement that those who do the highest good in this world are the ones who think the most of the next world? ❏ Yes ❏ No

List three people, famous or known only to you, who are doing good in this world.

_____

_____

_____

List three people who appear to be doing evil.

_____

_____

_____

Mark the list containing the people with the greatest regard for heaven.

Sojourners who think the most of the next world are usually those who are doing the highest good in this one.

The voices of this world have fooled many into believing the myth of "too heavenly minded to be of any earthly good."

Is it just possible that the voices of this world have fooled many into believing the myth of "too heavenly minded to be of any earthly good?"

 Check each of the following statements that will be results when a Christian begins to realize his or her citizenship is in heaven.

❑ He begins acting as a responsible citizen of earth.
❑ She invests wisely in relationships because she knows they're eternal.
❑ His conversations, goals, and motives become pure and honest because he realizes these will have a bearing on everlasting reward.
❑ She gives generously of time, money, and talent because she's laying up treasures for eternity.
❑ He spreads the good news of Christ because he longs to fill heaven's ranks with his friends and neighbors.

You could well have checked each of the statements. The believer with a view toward heaven will seek to follow each of these values. All this serves the pilgrim well not only in heaven, but on earth; for it serves everyone around him.

A few weeks ago I went to the Hair and Nail Shoppe to get a haircut. As the stylist whipped the plastic cape over me, I glanced around at the other women. Ladies sat under hair dryers absorbed in *Vogue* magazines. A few women gabbed with their manicurists about the latest shades of red nail polish. I looked on either side of me: a redhead in jeans was cracking gum and cutting the locks of the lady to my right, while a short Asian woman with long black hair worked to the left.

What does a pilgrim do in an average ordinary place like this? (At least average and ordinary for southern California.) Sojourners look for the unseen divine realities around them. I tried to put myself in the shoes of these women, looking for their "realities"—divorce, dieting, raising children, running for the school board, fighting off alcoholism, or planning the next party. A few professional types in their power suits were dealing with different "realities"—promotions, payoffs, and executive stress.

Because faith helped me see each woman as precious in His sight, I knew God had His own divine realities in mind for each woman. I could pray, "Thy kingdom come, Thy will be done in the *Hair and Nail Shoppe* as it is in heaven."

So, sitting with my hair all wet, I interceded off and on for each person, setting in motion God's powerful workings in their lives. All because of faith. This is the way ordinary pilgrims make themselves of some earthly good.

My husband Ken lives like this. He's been fostering a relationship with two young gas-station attendants from Iran who work at the Shell station down the road. Most people are in and out for a quick fill-up, but Ken keeps his eyes open for the unseen divine realities at work in the lives of these two men. We're convinced that time, prayer, friendship, and a Bible in the Farsi language will make a difference. He's one heaven-minded person looking for ways to do earth some good.

Besides this, pilgrims do battle. The spiritual war raged hot and heavy earlier this year when Ken and I helped chaperone a high school prom. The early hours of the prom were a great time to connect with students and wish them well at college. After dinner, though, the lights went out, the music went up, and the ballroom reverted into a wild disco. I tried talking to my dinner partner, but we got tired of screaming at each other.

 If I stopped there, what ending could you attach to this story? I'm not looking for a "right" answer. Just describe in the margin some possible ways a heavenly-minded believer might be a positive influence in my situation.

Through the dark I spotted a senior girl in a white-sequined dress sitting on her boyfriend's knee. I decided to pray for her. As I stared at her, silently mouthing my prayer, it struck me that although the ballroom was shaking, my prayer was more powerful than the 600-amp speakers angled over the dance floor. A simple intercession was sending repercussions across heaven, as well as scattering a few demons. This is how heaven's citizens live while temporarily residing on earth. Heaven tells us every person, place, and thing has a purpose.

 The next time you are in an uncomfortable worldly situation, try interceding for those involved. Believe in the power of your prayer to scatter demons.

 You may not live in a world of senior proms. Think of several practical ways you could introduce some constructive heavenly-mindedness into your world this week. Be prepared to share these with your group.

We do not lose heart.. . . we fix our eyes not on what is seen, but what is unseen. For what is seen is temporary, but what is unseen is eternal.
—2 Corinthians 4:16, 18

Unit 5
Why Do We Fit in Heaven?

*T*ake a minute to consider a time when you were actually homesick. Not for heaven, but for your earthly home. Remember the aching? The sense of feeling like a stranger in your surroundings?

Boy, I remember it. I felt like my guts were being ripped out. I bawled when I was a little girl and had to stay at Aunt Dorothy's while my mother had a gallbladder operation. Then there was church camp. I was miserable. And that Thanksgiving when I first moved to California.

My most recent bout with homesickness was in Bucharest, Romania. It was the middle of the night. I knew I was an alien as soon as I wheeled into the musty hotel lobby. A single dangling light bulb cast long shadows over dusty sofas and lamps leftover from the fifties. Bullet holes pierced the concrete wall. Moths and exhaust fumes filtered in through the open door, and somebody screamed at a neighbor down the street.

I was tired, hungry, and dirty. There were no ramps for my wheelchair. I didn't fit in the bathroom. I didn't feel at home in the restaurant, which served tough meat swimming in oil and garlic. A radio featured Elvis Presley wailing "I Wanna Be Your Teddy Bear." Everything about the place—the language, the culture, and especially the bed pillow—made me long for Calabasas, California. It was awful. You've felt the same.

Why did Calabasas grip my heart? Was it the sidewalk ramps and curb-cuts? Radio stations playing newer tunes than Elvis hits? Superior restaurants? Why do I feel I fit in California and not in Romania?

Because home is where your heart is.

What You'll Learn in This Unit

In this unit you will discover why heaven is your real home. Heaven is our heart's desire. It is the ecstacy only hinted at in this life. That ecstacy is all wrapped up in the person of our Savior. In heaven we will celebrate Christ's coronation day!

Unit Scripture

Store up for yourselves treasures in heaven, where moth and rust do not destroy, and where thieves do not break in and steal. For where your treasure is, there your heart will be also.
—Matthew 6:20-21

Lesson 1

Heaven Is Our Heart's Desire

---

*T*his powerful truth needs to be elevated for a moment above the cross-stitched plaques on which we usually read it. Because if "home is where the heart is," then home must be more than the street address where you live. When you get homesick, your heart may tug for your own mattress and pillow, but this doesn't account for that gut-wrenching ache. What makes home is not a place, but who lives there. You feel at home when your heart is nestled near the one you love.

But sometimes, when you least expect it, even the people who make up home aren't enough. Sometimes when you're all tucked in with your own pillow and blanket, with the voice of the one you love close by, another kind of homesickness—a deeper kind—sneaks up on you.

Still Not Satisfied

Fragrant pine branches and the softness of falling snow. Cinnamon-spiced tea and vanilla candles. It was home at its 1957 best. Especially with a Christmas Eve visit from Uncle George and Aunt Kitty who, when she leaned down to give me a big hug, let me bury my nose in her fox stole scented with Evening in Paris perfume. Together, with the rest of the family in the candlelit living room, we sat on the couch and listened to Bing Crosby Christmas music on the radio. It was a quiet time. It was home.

Suddenly, out of nowhere, I was broadsided with homesickness. Good grief, there I was in the coziest of houses snug on the couch between people I loved, yet mantled with homesickness—a nostalgia for a different kind of home.

The next morning that sensitive longing retired in the presence of mundane things, and I became my ordinary self. It was Christmas Day. I shelved my fascination with the strange longing and rushed headlong into my pile of presents. I ripped open the paper of one gift and asked, "Is there more?" And then another gift, asking, "How many left?" and then after the final present, whined, "Is that all there is?" What was I looking for? Why wasn't I satisfied?

Throughout the day, I knew I was free to play with my toys, but occasionally I would leave my gifts, go upstairs to my room

What makes home is not a place, but who lives there.

and lean on the windowsill to gaze outside. What was I pining after? What did I want?

 Have you ever wanted a gift so much you could "taste it"—then received it only to discover it did not satisfy? Be prepared to share your story in your group this week.

What Do We Want?

When it comes to heaven, we are all children opening a thousand beautiful Christmas presents and asking after each one, "Is that all there is?"

In fact, when it comes to heaven, why don't you make a Christmas list—all the best joys, gifts, and presents that you imagine heaven will offer. Ask your heart the question: What do you want? There's no restrictions on the list. The sky's the limit. Would it be beauty or wealth? Fame? Driving a Ferrari?

Now imagine getting it all. How soon do you think you would grow restless? How soon before you would say, "Is that all there is?"

Try another list, a deeper one. Endless talks with Beethoven about scoring music or long chats with Mary Cassatt discussing French Impressionism. Strategizing football plays with Tom Landry. How about a fit, healthy body for all you who have disabilities? Running? Dancing? Cooking with Julia Child? Playing guitar with Eric Clapton? A good conscience, freedom, peace of mind? It might be a few more thousand years before these would bore you, but eventually even they would become ho-hum.

 Suppose a Christian friend came to you and said, "I just don't know what's wrong. I have all the success and security I've wanted, but I still have a restless ache inside. What is missing?" What have you learned about heaven that might answer your friend's question?

_____

_____

_____

Peggy Lee was on to something back in the sixties when she serenaded us, asking, "Is that all there is, my friend? Then let's keep dancing, let's break out the booze and have a ball, if that's

Imagine getting it all. How soon before you would say, "Is that all there is?"

all ... there is."[26] The song scared me then, and it scares me now. Is there *nothing* that will ultimately satisfy our hearts? Peter Kreeft suggests:

> *Can you imagine any heaven that would not eventually be a bore? If not, does that mean that every good thing must come to an end, even heaven? After eighty or ninety years most people are ready to die; will we feel the same after eighty or ninety centuries of heaven? ... If we don't want boredom in heaven, what do we want? If heaven is real, what real desire does it satisfy? We want a heaven without death and without boredom. But we cannot imagine such a heaven. How can we desire something we cannot imagine?*[27]

We cannot conjure up heaven in our minds because our desires go deeper than what our minds can imagine.

Thankfully, our hearts are always a beat ahead of our minds and bodies. Proverbs 4:23 is not off base when it says the heart goes deeper than the mind: "Above all else, guard your heart, for it is the wellspring of life." True, it also says the heart is desperately wicked, but that still demonstrates that it is the seat of deep passions. Important things happen in the heart. Out of it "flow the issues of life." We may have one foot here and the other in the hereafter, but our heart is often that part of us which tugs and pulls at that one foot stuck in the mud of earth, saying, "Get off of the earthly images, would you? Look, here's your other foot anyway. Up here is what you're longing for."

Really? Does our heart have the answer?

Does our heart have something to say in response to this haunting echo?

Can we trust our heart to really know what it wants?

 Find and circle what the Scriptures in the margin have in common.

When people approached Jesus with a need, it's curious that He often responded, "What do you want?" I've always thought this was an odd thing to say since, first, He could read their minds, and second, their need was often obvious—like Bartimaeus, the blind beggar, for one. But Jesus has His reasons for asking. He urges us to explore our heart's list of wants because He knows that we desire something deeper than getting a few surface needs satisfied.

Jesus stopped and called them. "What do you want me to do for you?" he asked.
—Matthew 20:32

"What do you want me to do for you?" he asked.
—Mark 10:36

Turning around, Jesus saw them following and asked, "What do you want?"
—John 1:38

And when it comes to heaven, He knows we desire something more fundamental than pleasure, prosperity, or power. Our heart thinks it's desperate to get back to the garden, or, if not there, then someplace where our innocence and identity are sequestered. Says C. S. Lewis:

> *Our lifelong nostalgia, our longing to be reunited with something in the universe from which we now feel cut off, to be on the inside of some door which we have always seen from the outside, is no mere neurotic fancy, but the truest index of our real situation ... at last to be summoned inside would be both glory and honor and also the healing of that old ache.*[28]

 How do you react to C. S. Lewis' suggestion that you have a deep yearning, too deep for words, an ache that only heaven can fill? Check any of the following or add your own.

❑ Yes, the ache is there. I just never put it into words before.
❑ I feel like I've climbed the ladder of success and found it leaning against the wrong wall.
❑ No, I have no ache in my life.
❑ I really don't understand what he is talking about
❑ Your response: _____

Read Jesus' words appearing in the margin. Thank Him for the areas of your life in which you feel a sense of fulfillment. Talk to Him about the ache only heaven will fill completely.

Lesson 2

Heaven Is Ecstasy

*W*hen attempting to heal that old ache of unfulfilled yearning, the human heart has had lots of experience. It is restless and raging, trying this and dabbling in that, hoping to possess something that will give us innocence, identity, and ... heaven. Our poor bruised heart, though, does not really want to

Whoever drinks the water I give him will never thirst. Indeed, the water I give him will become in him a spring of water welling up to eternal life."
—John 4:14

possess heaven so much as to be possessed by it. It desires not so much pleasure, for pleasure can be exhausted. After we experience it, it's over. Our heart wants something that lasts. For forever? Yes, if it were possible.

What the heart desires is ecstasy.

Ecstasy is that marvelous euphoria in which we totally forget ourselves and yet find ourselves. The dictionary describes it as a state of being overpowered by joy, which causes you to step outside yourself, and a subscript explains that in Greek ecstasy means to "stand outside oneself." But a powerful experience like this can't be defined by a dictionary. To appreciate its meaning, ecstasy has to be experienced.

 Think of the most ecstatic experience in your life. Imagine, that was a tiny little foretaste of what heaven will be like.

Ecstacy is rapturous delight. Intense joy. Pure passion. When it comes to heaven, we want to be overpowered and caught up in something grand and wonderful outside ourselves. We want to be swept and wrapped up in a joy that weaves itself through every nerve and fiber. A joy that makes time stand still. We want to lose all sense of time and, therefore, disappointment. Like Elijah in his chariot, we want to be captured and carried away.

This is what our heart wants. This would be heaven without boredom.

Last night I experienced a taste of heaven when I wheeled out to my backyard to look at the full moon. It shone perfectly round and pale white through a sheer curtain of high, thin clouds. A sprinkle of blue stars peeked through the haze, and someone down the street was playing a Chopin melody on a piano. A warm breeze touched me. A half-forgotten poem came to mind as I strained to see the stars: "They were tiny peepholes in a great black wall with the party lights of heaven streaming through."

For a split second I was in ecstasy. My heart broke for joy and then ... it was gone. Whenever we stumble upon ecstasy, our heart knows beyond a doubt that this is it. It's a glorious healing of that old ache, even if but for a short moment. Lovers who speak of being "in love" feel it most often. They stumble into love, lose themselves, and then find themselves overwhelmed by something gloriously larger that possesses them. And it's ecstatic.

Our heart wants something that lasts forever.

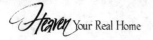

Romantic love is meant to point us to a greater, more fulfilling joy that enraptures.

You know what it's like. You know how it feels. Your heart grows faint and your breathing grows short just picturing the soft eyes and tender smile of the one you adore. Just being in the same room together is a thrill. You ply him with questions just to hear the sound of his voice. And the thought of a kiss? An embrace? You all but melt.

This kind of love, romantic love, is as close as many people get to the healing of that ache. Trouble is, most people forget that romantic love, like all the other loves—agape, phileo, or eros—is meant to point us to a greater, more fulfilling joy that enraptures. People cherish the glory they see in their lover, and they forget that the glory is not in the one they love, so much as shining through him or her. Most people are blind when it comes to this. They don't realize that all the glory comes from beyond the one being cherished, like a light reflecting in a mirror. They make the mistake of idolizing the one by whom they are smitten, rather than reading the cues that keep whispering, "It's not me … it's not in my eyes … I'm only a reminder of something, Someone else. Quick, who do I remind you of? Here's a hint: I'm made in the image of God."

Most people never take this broad and glorious hint. They forget that the human soul was made to enjoy some object never given, but only alluded to. They forget and so they place in the hands of the one they love the incredible burden of keeping the cup of joy overflowing; they heap on the lover's shoulders the weight of sustaining ecstasy that only God can carry.

 Have you or anyone you know ever expected a romantic relationship to do the impossible—to stay in a state of continual ecstacy? ❏ Yes ❏ No If so, describe what resulted.

_____

_____

So frequently people expect another human, especially a husband or wife, to supply what comes only from God. They think that romantic love truly can "conquer all." The result? They are bitterly crushed when romance fades and the one they adore fails to be God, falling short of keeping them enraptured. And so, on to the next lover. And the next god. And the next.[29]

Christians are rightfully coaxed in 1 Peter 1:22 to "love one another other deeply, from the heart." And for good reasons.

In the first place, Christians get the hint, recognize the cues, and understand that the person we love is stamped with the image of God. We have the "homing detector," the flight instruments to help us see that the converging points in eternity do not meet in the face of the one we love, but pass through to meet in the face of God. To love each other deeply is to acknowledge that the divine glory that we see in the eyes of another is a reflection from beyond. This makes Christian love all the sweeter and each friend is an open invitation to see Jesus in him or her. As the song goes:

I see Jesus in your eyes and it makes me love Him,
I feel Jesus in your touch and I know He cares,
I hear Jesus in your voice and it makes me listen.[30]

What's more, the love Christians share lasts much longer than any old romance. It lasts longer than a lifetime.

Second, we have a built-in warning system that sounds an alarm if we start to idolize the one we love. It blares, "Wrong coordinates! The points converge not in this face, but in God's! Get back on track!" God wants us to learn that human love is a signpost pointing to divine love. We are to learn where love's focus should be, and not be like a puppy dog who wags his tail and sniffs your finger when you are trying to point him to his food. Christians can and should properly read the signs. The one we love is a gift from God and, as a gift, points us to the Giver who is the One and only One who can provide an overflowing cup of joy, if not occasional ecstasy. This warning system keeps love, whether for our husband, wife, or friend, rightly focused and constantly refreshed.

Human love is a signpost pointing to divine love.

 How can you know when your love for another person begins to cross the line and become idolatry? Here is a checklist. Check the ones you recognize—that you have seen in yourself or in someone else.

❑ Expectations: "You are supposed to make me happy."
❑ Pedestals: "You are perfect; you can do no wrong."
❑ Distortion of Attention: "You are all I think about."
❑ Denial: "I know you'll never let me down."

Third, and most important, when we Christians love each other deeply, we catch a glimpse of that particular facet of God's love that is being cut, honed, and shaped in the lives of the ones we deeply love. We savor a foretaste of their true identities reserved in heaven, we inhale the fragrance of the heavenly persons they are becoming. We see a particular aspect of heaven in them. We rejoice, and God receives glory—the mirror reflects His image back to Himself. Once again, we are reminded that one day in eternity He shall indeed "be all and in all."

C. S. Lewis was intimately acquainted with the way humans mirror a higher, more heavenly glory when he wrote, "Remember that the dullest and most uninteresting person you talk to may one day be a creature which, if you saw it now, you would be strongly tempted to worship."[31]

For me, this is one of those unseen divine realities. Within our heart we find a shadow of heaven, especially as we "love one another deeply," for love is an unconscious desire for heaven. We now know what we want. We know the answer to our heart's longing.

 Pray for the discernment to recognize the face of God behind the faces of people in your relationships.

Love is an unconscious desire for heaven.

Lesson 3

Heaven Is a Person

*W*hat you do find in your heart and what you see reflected in the ones you love is God. He and He alone provides the healing of that old ache. That's why heaven has to be more than a place.

Much, much more.

It must be a Person.

If you need a bit more convincing, then take this test St. Augustine gave his students centuries ago. Imagine God appeared to you and said, "You want heaven? I'll make a deal with you. I'll give you anything and everything you ask. Nothing will be a sin; nothing will be forbidden; and nothing will be impossible for you. You will never be bored and you will never die. Only ... you shall never see my face."[32]

Brrrr! Do you feel that chill in your soul? Your heart and mind recoil in unison on this one. Your primordial desire is that you want God more than anything else in the world. Like St.

Augustine said, "Thou hast made us for thyself, and therefore our hearts are restless until they rest in thee."[33]

Yes, your heart's home is in the heart of God. He has placed within you a yearning for Himself, a desire to know Him and understand what He is like. Every soul feels the void and the emptiness until it connects with its Maker.

Pleasures and treasures on earth may be sought after and not found, but only God comes with the guarantee that He will be found. "'You will seek me and find me when you seek me with all your heart. I will be found by you,' declares the Lord, 'and will bring you back from captivity'" (Jeremiah 29:13-14). Hurrah, no more exile! No more strangers in a strange land! God assures us "I will be found by you."

 Read John 14:9 in the margin. How has Jeremiah 29:13-14 been fulfilled?

_____

_____

Jesus answered ... "Anyone who has seen me has seen the Father."
—John 14:9

Specifically, God will be found in Jesus Christ. He illumines our hearts and minds when we sincerely search for the Truth. He reveals Jesus, the photo image of the Father who dwells in unapproachable light. Jesus is the source of the haunting echo and the heavenly song. Jesus is God wearing a human face. He is real and not abstract. He invites us to do what we cannot do with the Incomprehensible—He invites us to drink and eat of Him, and "taste and see that the Lord is good" (Psalm 34:8).

Jesus is sunshine to our hearts. Not just to our logic, but our hearts. Praise God, we know the answer to our hearts' longing. It's Jesus!

The disciples of Jesus, at first, weren't so sure that this Man in their midst would fulfill their deepest longings, so "Philip said, 'Lord, show us the Father and that will be enough for us.' Jesus answered: 'Don't you know me, Philip, even after I have been among you such a long time? Anyone who has seen me has seen the Father'" (John 14:8-9).

Our longings are satisfied in Him for "the Son is the radiance of God's glory and the exact representation of his being" (Hebrews 1:3). We can know God—our Father in heaven—if we know Jesus. And knowing Him, as we would desire to know a Lover, is ecstasy. His invitation to "enter into the joy of the Lord" is like stepping into a raft and being carried helpless-

ly along a surging current, spilling over and splashing with joy. Please note that the joy of the Lord does not enter into us, but we, into it. We are enveloped by something larger, something greater than ourselves, a heavenly "in-loveness" in which we can do nothing but laugh and enjoy the ride. Jesus smiles, stretches out His hand and welcomes us into His raft with the invitation, "whoever loses his life for my sake will find it" (Matthew 10:39).

 If you have a love relationship with Jesus, how does it affect your use of time? your interests? your priorities?

_____

_____

In what ways is a relationship with Jesus like the human experience of being "in love"?

_____

_____

In what ways is it different?

_____

_____

Face-to-Face

Remember when I shared that lovers always focus on the face of the one they adore? And in that face they find ecstasy, albeit fleeting?

 Here's a pop quiz for all you romantics: In whose face do we find lasting ecstasy? Take a broad and glorious hint from Psalm 27:4, 8.

_____

And if you need another reminder, listen to Psalm 105:4: "Look to the Lord and his strength; seek his face always." The points of eternity converge in the face of our Savior.

Since you got the answer to that question, this next one is easy: What are the correct coordinates for focusing your faith?

One thing I ask of the Lord, this is what I seek: that I may dwell in the house of the Lord all the days of my life, to gaze upon the beauty of the Lord. My heart says of you, "Seek his face!" Your face, Lord, I will seek.
—Psalm 27:4, 8

The faith of which I have been speaking up until now is only the lens, the spectacles through which "the eyes of the heart may be enlightened" (Ephesians 1:18). The faith I've been describing is only a way of seeing and, therefore, believing something. But this isn't the whole story.

The correct coordinates on which to focus the eyes of the heart are Hebrews 12:2: "Let us fix our eyes on Jesus, the author and perfecter of our faith." Jesus is the Unseen Divine Reality. Everything shall find its future divine fulfillment in Him. "For no matter how many promises God has made, they are 'Yes' in Christ," says 2 Corinthians 1:20. This means every promise. The Author and Perfecter has conceived every unseen divine purpose and has planned its fulfillment to be a part of the wonder of heaven, "so that in everything he might have the supremacy" (Colossians 1:18).

Everything from Pikes Peak to my backyard washed in the glow of a full moon—every bit of beauty here is but a shadow of something far more beautiful there, and "we know that the whole creation has been groaning as in the pains of childbirth right up to the present time" (Romans 8:22). The creation is groaning, longing to be clothed with the beauty its Designer originally intended.

 Here's a heavenly treasure hunt. In the margin list the treasures you will receive in completed form in heaven. I've named several in the paragraphs below.

Not only this dusty little planet will find fulfillment but, we will, for "we ourselves, who have the firstfruits of the Spirit, groan inwardly as we wait eagerly for our adoption as sons" (Romans 8:23).

He will give us much more than the innocence we were groping for back in the garden; He has imputed to us His righteousness. Our future divine fulfillment is alluded to in 1 John 3:2: "We know that when he appears, we shall be like him, for we shall see him as he is." Completely.

To pursue heaven is to pursue Him. To pursue Him is to find heaven.

It's that simple. If you wholeheartedly pursue Jesus, you can't help but be heaven-minded and sigh with Psalm 73:25: "Whom have I in heaven but you? And earth has nothing I desire besides you."

Some will say, though, "Wait a minute, there are a lot of other things on earth I desire. Besides, I already know Jesus,

I'm saved—have been for 15 years—but I'm still not gripped by heavenly glories above. I'm still not homesick for heaven."

🕊 **Does that last paragraph still describe your feelings? Does your "heavenly homesickness" need to grow? May I suggest that you make Psalm 73:25 your prayer? Carry it with you. Memorize those words. Keep praying that simple prayer, and see what happens.**

Whom have I in heaven but you? And earth has nothing I desire besides you.
—Psalm 73:25:

Lesson 4

Heaven Is the Home of Love

To think about heaven is to think about Jesus. To pursue heaven with your heart is to pursue Him.

I'm not taking literary license. I'm not being lazy with biblical interpretations. Heaven and God are intimately entwined, and the pursuit of one is the pursuit of the other. Matthew 23:22 says, "He who swears by heaven swears by God's throne and by the one who sits on it." If you swear by heaven, you are swearing by God. Heaven is the place where God is, so that you can refer to one or the other and virtually mean both.

Whenever Scripture refers to the kingdom of heaven, it means the kingdom of God. John MacArthur explains:

It's just another way to express God. In the period between the Old and New Testament, the Jews never used the name of God ... because they thought it was too holy to come through their lips. One of the things they substituted for the name of God was heaven. Instead of saying, "I worship God," they would say, "I worship heaven." Instead of saying, "Call upon the name of God," they would say, "Call upon the name of heaven." To enter the kingdom of heaven is to enter the kingdom of God.[34]

The King of heaven wants us to see this tight connection between the Place and the Person. When our heart melts into God's and when our mind is thinking on Him, Place and Person no longer seem separated. "God [has] raised us up with Christ and seated us with him in the heavenly realms in Christ Jesus" (Ephesians 2:6). Amazing!

When we understand our position in Christ, we begin to grasp our position in the heavenly realms. We are already seated with Christ in the heavenly realms. I'm not talking about astral projection or anything spooky. We're not actually in heaven the place, yet. But we are in the heavenly realms in that it's a sphere in which we live under God's rule and His Spirit's blessing. We are under the dominion of the King of heaven, and that places us in His realm. The King has come as well as His kingdom. The King is in our midst, and His kingdom is within us. All signs point to there and here. All signs lead to Him because all signs come from Him.

 In the margin read Hebrews 12:22-23. Use your eyes of faith here. This is another one of those unseen divine realities. Why do you suppose all the verbs are in the present tense?

_____

_____

> *You have come to Mount Zion, to the heavenly Jerusalem, the city of the living God. You have come to thousands upon thousands of angels in joyful assembly, to the church of the firstborn, whose names are written in heaven.*
> *—Hebrews 12:22-23*

As I said in an earlier chapter, present tense may have something to do with the different kind of time in which heaven exists, or the next and new dimension of mansions and golden streets. More likely, God simply wants to get your mind racing and your heart beating with a right-around-the-corner anticipation of heaven. Isn't that the way strangers on foreign soil are supposed to feel about their homeland?

 What practical difference do you suppose living in the present tense regarding heaven—seeing yourself as already seated together with Christ in heavenly places—will make in your life? See if your responses match any of the ones I've named in the paragraphs below.

Live in the present tense of heaven and you will smell the heavenly fragrance of the person you will become. Your life will have intensity and depth. You will sit close to self-scrutiny, understanding that by your words and actions you are doing earth a world of good. Your heaven-inspired faith will give you joy and peace, without parade or noise.

Most of all, you will begin to feel at home. You will begin to see "our Father who art in heaven" not as the Incomprehensible, but as Jesus sees Him: Abba-Father. Daddy.

Home is where Daddy is.

In my Father's house are many rooms; if it were not so, I would have told you. I am going there to prepare a place for you. And if I go and prepare a place for you, I will come back and take you to be with me that you also may be where I am.
—John 14:2-3

The Lord will take delight in you. ... As a bridegroom rejoices over his bride, so will your God rejoice over you.
—Isaiah 62:4-5

Behold the Bridegroom!

John 3:29 tells me that "the bride belongs to the bridegroom," and, unlike the situation in modern marriages, I'm His possession. My life is hid with Christ in God, and who I am won't appear until He appears. My life is wrapped up in the One who redeemed me. Redeemed me in love. So, naturally I'm going to pine for Him and feel homesick to be with Him, especially when I know where He is and what He's doing.

 According to John 14:2-3, what is Jesus doing now?

_____

These are the words of a Lover. The Lover of my soul. Maybe at one time the meaning in this verse eluded me, but when placed in the context of Him as Bridegroom, and me as bride, it has me packing my trousseau and getting ready to go.

My love for heaven is energized because I know how He feels about me.

 Isaiah 62:4-5 appears in the margin. Circle the word that describes how Jesus feels about you.

Ponder that for a moment. He rejoices over you, and don't say that word like a plaster-of-paris saint in a less-than-amazing tone of voice. It's a jump-up-and-down, clenched fist, throw-your-head-back, and yell out loud, "Rejoice!" Jesus is brimming with heartfelt love for you.

It's not a matter of sweet words. No. He gave His life as His dowry, and the Cross shows me that He and His Father agreed on an exorbitant price. Every time I drink from the communion cup, I remember the covenant between my Bridegroom and me. And I've promised Him I will drink from that cup in remembrance of Him until He comes.

Until He comes. That's the hard part.

Waiting is so hard. It's even harder when you love someone.

Be Prepared ... the Pure and Spotless Bride

I want to see the face of my Savior. You may not realize it, but you do too. We want to see. We find it hard to rest comfortably in a relationship—with God, with anyone—when we cannot see the face of the one we adore. This is why I paint in my head the faces of friends I care deeply about, especially when I'm away from them. The essence of who they are is held in the eyes, the mouth, the smile. The face is the focal point of personality.

In the relationship between brides and bridegrooms, full intimacy comes between a man and a woman face-to-face. And when the Bible speaks of longing for God, it speaks in terms of wanting to see His face. The psalmist pleads with God, "Make your face shine upon us," and "Do not hide your face from us." Ultimately, "in righteousness I will see your face; when I awake, I will be satisfied with seeing your likeness" (Psalm 17:15).

To hold the gaze of God is to find love, acceptance, and satisfaction.

🕊 Like the psalmist, look forward to that moment when you will see the face of your Bridegroom Jesus. Express to Him your feelings about seeing Him face-to-face.

To hold the gaze of God is to find love, acceptance, and satisfaction.

Lesson 5

Heaven Is Christ's Coronation

Holy, Holy, Holy! All the saints adore Thee,
Casting down their golden crowns
*   around the glassy sea;*
Cherubim and Seraphim falling down before Thee,
Which wert and art and evermore shall be.[35]

Heaven will be Christ's coronation day. I'm thrilled that we will enjoy the marriage supper of the Lamb with its feast of rich foods, and we will delight in our reunion with loved ones. Yes, it will be exhilarating to reign over angels and rule the earth with new bodies to boot. But I have to keep remembering it will not be our celebration. It will be His.

We shall press in line with the great procession of the redeemed passing before the throne, an infinite cavalcade of nations and empires, all standing shoulder-to-shoulder, generations of the redeemed before the cross and after, all bearing their diadems before God Almighty.

Then as Jesus rises from His throne before this great host, all crowns are lifted, all chimes are ringing, and all hallelujahs are hailing until the vocabulary of heavenly praise is exhausted. We

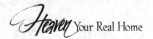

will press our crowns against our breasts, look at one another, and say, "Now?"

"Now!" all will shout. Together we will raise our voices, not in four-part harmony, but perhaps in twelve-part, with the twenty-four elders as "they lay their crowns before the throne" (Revelation 4:10) and sing:

> Crown Him with many crowns,
>   the Lamb upon His throne:
> Hark! How the heavenly anthem
>   drowns all music but its own!
> Awake, my soul and sing
>   of Him who died for thee,
> And hail Him as thy matchless King
>   through all eternity.[36]

If, indeed, we are given literal crowns, make no mistake about it—the diadems will be His. The judgment seat of Christ may have been center stage where Jesus showered praise on the believer, but all of heaven will turn the spotlight on the Lord to give Him back the glory. The universe will bow its knee and hail Jesus as King of kings and Lord of lords when He raises His sword in victory over death, the devil, disease, and destruction.

This is what I was made for. This is the answer to all the times I asked on earth, "Why has God chosen me? Why not someone else?" The response is simply, I am the Father's gift to the Son. Ephesians 1:11-12 will then make perfect sense for "in him we were chosen ... in order that we ... might be for the praise of his glory." I will be the flashing and iridescent gift for the Son whom Zechariah admired, "They will sparkle in his land like jewels in a crown. How attractive and beautiful they will be!" (Zechariah 9:16-17).

Earth was one big diamond mine in which I was chiseled from the dirt, cleaned, polished, and fitted for a King's crown. Can you now understand why I want to win as many crowns as possible while on earth? The more crowns, the merrier God's praise. My motive in gathering a truckload of diadems is not to hoard them, but to have more to cast at Jesus' feet.

You and I were chosen to praise Him. It's that simple. What a shame that on earth we made it so complicated.

In the early days of my paralysis when I first learned about heaven, I zeroed in on it because it was the place where I would receive new hands and feet. Heaven was the place I'd be freed

I want to win as many crowns as possible to have more to cast at Jesus' feet.

from the pain, and so, it became an escape from reality. A psychological crutch. At times, heaven was so me-centered that I felt as though the whole point of it was to get back all it owed me, all I had lost. And so, heaven became a death wish.

 Do you identify with me in this selfish view of heaven? Was your attitude about heaven once mostly "me-centered"? How has your attitude about heaven changed?

_____

_____

Time passed, and with it I gained a little more spiritual maturity. It gradually dawned on me that the day of Christ would be just that ... the day of Christ, not the day of Joni. Glorified hands and feet, as well as reunions with loved ones, began to look more like fringe benefits to the honor of simply being on the invitation list to the coronation party.

You'll agree. The privilege of casting your crowns at the feet of Jesus will be enough of an honor. Ruling the earth and reigning over angels, becoming pillars in God's temple and co-heirs of heaven and earth are almost incidental. What we become, receive, and do in heaven won't be the highlight of heaven. To be there and to exist for the praise of His glory will be enough.

It will be Jesus' day.

Jesus Is Lord!

We should have known it all along. But it never sunk in. Oh, we understood it on paper, but how often did we live—really live—with the focus off ourselves and fixed on Christ as King of kings? It takes heaven to force us to fully comprehend what should have been plain on earth all along. If only we had stopped and read—really read—that "the God who made the world and everything in it is the Lord of heaven and earth" (Acts 17:24).

Jesus is the Lord of heaven and earth.

How often did we live with the focus off ourselves and fixed on Christ as King?

 Before you read on, explain what it means to you to call Jesus Lord.

_____

_____

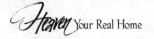

We said it in our prayers, we sang it in our songs, and we would have sworn we believed it with a capital *B*. But it never really clicked for us. That's because "us" kept getting in the way. All those years when earthly trials hit hard, we burnt rubber in our brains trying to figure out what it meant to us. How problems fit into God's plan for us. How Jesus could be conformed in us. Everything was always "for us." Even Sunday worship service focused on how we felt, what we learned, and if the hymns were to our liking.

While on earth, you never could have convinced us. We acted more like His kingdom sort of came, but not really. We behaved like His will was done on-earth-as-it-is-in-heaven mainly to benefit our jobs and relationships. And whenever we talked about heaven, it was more along the lines of an eternal playground where we would receive lots of new toys while God, like a granddaddy, would nod and smile to see us enjoying ourselves.

What a shame that on earth we acted as though we did God a big favor by accepting Jesus as Savior. We pitied Jesus because His reputation could never quite be vindicated. We felt sorry for God because it seemed like His justice was never quite served; in fact, at times we were embarrassed for our "King" as we scrambled to defend Him over earthly holocausts and horrors. Jesus never appeared to flex His kingly muscles, and thus never got credit, much less glory.

We weren't the only shortsighted ones. Even the disciples had a small-minded view of God. They too failed to recognize the King in their midst. Occasionally the fog lifted from their thinking, and once, toward the end of Jesus' ministry, they rose to a heavenly perspective of their King and said, "Now we can see that you know all things." For a brief moment, their focus was off the kingdom on earth and fixed on the kingdom in heaven. It was a rare flash of revelation, and Jesus was moved enough to exclaim, "You believe at last!" (John 16:30-31).

 According to John 6:28-29, what does God want from us?

_____

Those words of Christ rip at my heart. All Jesus wanted from us was, at last to believe. So why were our times of drastic obedience and absolute trust only flashes, brief moments of illumination? Why did we always have such a hard time acting like Jesus was King?

Why, oh why, didn't we take the hint from Acts 17:24-25 and switch our attention off us and onto Him? Why didn't we appreciate that God gave every trial, heartache, and happiness to show us something about Himself?

That we might appreciate His grace?

That we were being polished for the praise of His glory?

That we might see that everything fit together in order that we might know Him?

We always marvel that God shows an interest in us, but in heaven it will be clear that every earthly thing happened so that we'd show an interest in Him. In every trial, happiness, and heartache, God wanted us to think about Him. We will finally be convinced that the One whom we lauded with our lips as King truly did have supremacy in all things.

His kingdom came.

His will was done on earth as it is in heaven.

His word went forth and accomplished His purposes.

He was sovereign Lord over all.

The God who made the world and everything in it is the Lord of heaven and earth and does not live in temples built by hands. And he is not served by human hands, as if he needed anything, because he himself gives all men life and breath and everything else.
—Acts 17:24-25

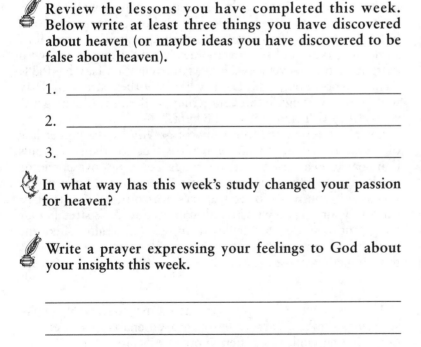

Review the lessons you have completed this week. Below write at least three things you have discovered about heaven (or maybe ideas you have discovered to be false about heaven).

1. _____

2. _____

3. _____

In what way has this week's study changed your passion for heaven?

Write a prayer expressing your feelings to God about your insights this week.

_____

_____

_____

Unit 6

How Does Heaven Help Me Handle Today?

Hardships are God's way of helping me get my mind on the hereafter. I don't mean the hereafter as a death wish, psychological crutch, or escape from reality. I mean "hereafter" as the true reality. Heaven is a glorious vantage point from which to look down on my pain and problems.

It's odd that it took a wheelchair—something that bolts me to earth—to make me see the futility of fighting spiritual battles on the earthly plane. When I attempted to live on the same low level as my bolts, gears, wheels, and leather, I made blunder after blunder. I was powerless there until I shifted to a higher battleground and chose a different perspective.

Looking down on my problems from heaven's perspective, trials looked extraordinarily different. When viewed from its own level, my paralysis seemed like a huge, impassable wall; but when viewed from above, the wall appeared as a thin line, something that could be overcome. It was, I discovered with delight, a bird's-eye view. It was the view of Isaiah 40:31: "Those who hope in the Lord will renew their strength. They will soar on wings like eagles; they will run and not grow weary, they will walk and not be faint."

Eagles overcome the lower law of gravity by the higher law of flight, and what is true for birds is true for the soul. Souls that soar to heaven's heights on wings like eagles overcome the mud of earth that keeps us stuck to a temporal, limited perspective. If you want to see heaven's horizons, as well as place earth in your rearview mirror, all you need to do is stretch your wings and consider your trials from heaven's realms. Like the wall that becomes a thin line, you are able to see the other side, the happier outcome.

What You'll Learn in This Unit

This week we will explore the awesome mystery of human suffering. While we are on earth, heaven enables us to endure our suffering while our suffering prepares us for heaven.

Unit Scripture

I consider that our present sufferings are not worth comparing with the glory that will be revealed in us. —Romans 8:18

Lesson 1

Suffering Is Momentary

Scripture mainly presents us with a view of life from the eternal perspective. Some call it "the heavenly point of view." I like to refer to it as the "end-of-time view." This perspective separates what is transitory from what is lasting.

What is transitory, such as physical pain, will not endure. What is lasting, such as the eternal weight of glory accrued from that pain, will remain forever. Everything else—numbing heartache, deep disappointment, circumstances that seem topsy-turvy—everything else, no matter how real it seems to us on earth, is treated as inconsequential. Hardships are hardly worth noticing. Every time my corset wears a wound in my side or I'm faced with a four-week stint in bed or I feel the stab of someone else's pity, I look beyond the negatives and see the positives.

 Practice thinking from the "end-of-time" perspective. Mark each of the following either E for eternal or T for temporal.

___ arthritis	___ cancer
___ heartache	___ God's word
___ love	___ envy
___ praise	___ hunger
___ wealth	___ joy

The apostle Paul had an eternal perspective when he said, "For our light and momentary troubles are achieving for us an eternal glory that far outweighs them all" (2 Corinthians 4:17). And regarding his own problems, he added, "I consider them rubbish" (Philippians 3:7).

Wait a minute. Did he say, "Troubles, light"? "Hardships, rubbish"?

The apostle Peter had this perspective too when he wrote to Christian friends being flogged and beaten. "In this you greatly rejoice, though now for a little while you may have had to suffer grief in all kinds of trials" (1 Peter 1:6).

Rejoice? When you're being thrown to lions? The Christians to whom Peter was writing were suffering horribly under Nero,

The "end-of-time view" separates what is transitory from what is lasting.

the Roman emperor. Peter expected them to view their problems as lasting a little while? What sort of watch was he using?

 Name three things that trouble you now but that will not pass the "end-of-time" test.

1. _____

2. _____

3. _____

This kind of nonchalance about gut-wrenching suffering used to drive me crazy. Stuck in a wheelchair and staring out the window over the fields of our farm, I wondered, *Lord, how in the world can You consider my troubles light and momentary? I will never walk or run again. I will never use my hands; I've got a leaky leg bag; I smell like urine; my back aches; and I'm trapped in front of this window. Maybe You see all of this achieving an eternal glory, but all I see is one awful day after the next in this stinking wheelchair!*

I did not buy the heavenly point of view. My pain screamed for my undivided attention, insisting, "Forget the future! What's God going to do now?" Time does that. It rivets your attention on temporal things and makes you live in the moment. And suffering doesn't make it any easier. It tightens the screw on the moment, making you anxious to find quick fix-its or escape hatches.

That's what it was like as I pitied myself in my chair. When I read Romans 5:3, "rejoice in our sufferings," my first thought was, *Sure, God, I'll rejoice the day You get me out of this thing!* And if You don't, what's going on? Are You poking fun at my paralysis? Trying to convince me I'm in spiritual denial? That my hurt and pain are imaginary? When it came to my affliction being light and momentary, God was obviously using a different dictionary.

 Before you read on, how would you answer the questions I was asking?

_____

_____

Time rivets your attention on temporal things and makes you live in the moment.

Years later the light dawned. The Lord hadn't used a different lexicon when He picked words like "light and momentary" to define earthly troubles. Even if it meant being sawed asunder, torn apart by lions, or plopped in a wheelchair for life, the Spirit-inspired writers of the Bible simply had a different perspective, an end-of-time view. Tim Stafford says, "This is why Scripture can seem at times so blithely and irritatingly out of touch with reality, brushing past huge philosophical problems and personal agony. But that is just how life is when you are looking from the end. Perspective changes everything. What seems so important at the time has no significance at all."[37]

It's a matter of perspective. What could possibly outweigh the pain of permanent paralysis? The coordinates of the new perspective are found in 2 Corinthians 4:18, "So we fix our eyes not on what is seen, but on what is unseen. For what is seen is temporary, but what is unseen is eternal."

The greater weight of eternal glory is clear: Knowing Christ fully, my King and co-heir. The final destruction of death, disease, and the devil. The vindication of His holy name. The restoration of all things under Christ.

These things outweigh my thousands of afternoons of painful discomfort and high blood pressure any day. They outweigh a lifetime of not feeling or moving. Mind you, I'm not saying that my paralysis is light in and of itself; it only becomes light in contrast to the far greater weight on the other side of the scale. Although I wouldn't normally call three decades in a wheelchair "momentary," it is when you realize that "you are a mist that appears for a little while and then vanishes" (James 4:14).

 Think of a painful experience that seemed like an eternity at the time but now from the perspective of today seems like a blip on the screen of your life.

Scripture is constantly trying to get us to look at life this way. Our life is but a blip on the eternal screen. Pain will be erased by a greater understanding; it will be eclipsed by a glorious result. Something so superb, so grandiose is going to happen at the world's finale, that it will suffice for every hurt and atone for every heartache. The state of suffering we are in here is necessary to reach the state we want (God wants!) in heaven.

Jesus spent so much energy emphasizing the end-of-time perspective because He had come from heaven, and He knew how wonderful it was. Thus, He was always focusing on end results — the harvest of the crop, the fruit from the tree, the

Therefore we do not lose heart. Though outwardly we are wasting away, yet inwardly we are being renewed day by day. For our light and momentary troubles are achieving for us an eternal glory that far outweighs them all.
—2 Corinthians 4:16-17

Jesus, who had come from heaven and knew how wonderful it was, always focused on end results.

close of the day's labor, the profit from the investment, the house that stands the storm. He knew if we were to rejoice in our suffering, our fascination with the here and now would have to be subdued. How else could He say to those who mourn, "You are blessed"? How else could He tell the persecuted to be happy? How else could He remind His followers facing torture and death to "count it all joy"?

Nothing more radically altered the way I looked at my suffering than leapfrogging to this end-of-time vantage point. Heaven became my greatest hope. In fact, I wondered how other people could possibly face quadriplegia, cancer, or even a death in the family without the hope of heaven. It meant no more wallowing away hours by the farmhouse window, scorning Romans 8:28, and muttering, "How can it say all things fit together into a pattern for good in my life!" God's pattern for my earthly good may have smelled like urine and felt painful, but I knew the end result in heaven would exude a fragrant and glorious aroma: Christ in me, the hope of glory.

Although paralysis has aided me in my pilgrimage, it has not made me automatically holy. You could say the same about your own suffering. Pain and problems do not make one instantly obedient. For me, it has taken time.

It's all a matter of time. God makes all things beautiful in His time according to Ecclesiastes 3:11. And for many, they won't see the beauty until the end of time. An end-of time perspective solves the dilemma of Romans 8:28, as well as all the other problems of evil, suffering, and pain.

God makes all things beautiful in His time.

 Pray for a concern you want God to make beautiful in His time. Thank Him in advance for His answer.

Lesson 2

Suffering Moves Our Heart Toward Heaven

Y*ou may not be paralyzed with a broken neck, but you could be paralyzed by other limitations. A broken heart. A broken home. A broken reputation. These things that presently scream for your undivided attention may close the doors to earthly satisfaction, but they can swing windows wide-open to a spirited hope of heaven.

Mind you, the closed doors—many of which have slammed in your face and crunched your fingers—are no accident. God wishes to instill within you a deep desire for your inheritance. In order to grip your heart, He will take drastic measures. You may not appreciate His method at first, but with an end-of-time perspective, you can be grateful for it. Samuel Rutherford described heaven and hardships this way:

> *If God had told me some time ago that He was about to make me as happy as I could be in this world, and then had told me that He should begin by crippling me in arm or limb, and removing me from all my usual sources of enjoyment, I should have thought it a very strange mode of accomplishing His purpose. And yet, how is His wisdom manifest even in this! For if you should see a man shut up in a closed room, idolizing a set of lamps and rejoicing in their light, and you wished to make him truly happy, you would begin by blowing out all his lamps; and then throw open the shutters to let in the light of heaven.*[38]

When an accident sent a broken neck my way, God blew out the lamps in my life that made the here and now so captivating. The despair of total and permanent paralysis that followed wasn't much fun, but it sure made heaven come alive. One day, when our Bridegroom comes back, there's not a doubt I'll be more excited and ready for it than if I were on my feet.

Suffering is no failure of God's plan. True, it is part of the curse, along with death, disease, and destruction. But before God comes back to close the curtain on suffering, it is meant to be redeemed. As Dorothy Sayers said, "Only in Christianity do we see a good God reaching down into what otherwise would be awful evil and wrench out of it positive good for us, and glory for Himself."

Suffering is no failure of God's plan.

 How would you describe to a hostile and skeptical world this connection between heaven and suffering?

_____

_____

_____

Earth can never meet your deepest longings.

Suffering makes us want to go to heaven. Broken homes and broken hearts crush our illusions that earth can keep its promises, that it can really satisfy. Only the hope of heaven can truly move our passions off this world—which God knows could never fulfill us anyway—and place them where they will find their glorious fulfillment.

When I was on my feet, it would have been nice had I focused on heaven purely for Christ's sake. Realistic? No. I was healthy, athletic, distracted, and not the type to get hyped about heaven for anyone's sake other than my own. Who wants to think about heaven when you've got things to do and places to go here? Besides, you have to die in order to get there. I did not want to think about that at the age of 17.

It's the nature of the human beast. At least this beast. Some people have to break their necks in order to get their hearts on heavenly glories above, and I happen to be one of them. Heaven interested me only after the permanency of my paralysis sank in.

You don't have to break your neck to get grabbed. When you come to know that the hopes you have cherished will never come true, that your loved one is gone from this life forever, that you will never be as pretty or successful or famous as you had once imagined, your sights are lifted. You long and look forward to the day when your hopes will be fulfilled and heartache will vanish. The glorious day when "we will be whole" becomes your passion as you realize that, once and for all, earth can never meet your deepest longings.

 On the following scale place an X at the spot to indicate to what degree earth has met your deepest longings.

0%   100%

 Now on the same scale place a ✓ to show to what degree you agree with the statement, "Only heaven can meet my deepest needs and desires."

You can appreciate that only heaven can meet your deepest needs, especially if earth has broken your heart. You may be a mother who has lost her child in an accident, a son who has lost his father to cancer, or a husband whose wife has passed on to glory. These dear ones take with them a part of your heart that no one can replace. Since the pursuit of heaven is an occupation of the heart anyway, don't be surprised if you find yourself longing for heaven after you leave the graveside. If your heart is with your loved ones, and they are home with the Lord, then heaven is home for you too.

A broken heart leads to the true contentment of asking less of this life because more is coming in the next. The art of living with suffering is the art of readjusting your expectations in the here and now. There are simply some things I will never have because of this wheelchair. Such longings heighten my loneliness here on earth.

 Write a paraphrase of Psalm 73:25-26 expressing your longing for God.

_____

_____

_____

Whom have I in heaven but you? And earth has nothing I desire besides you. My flesh and my heart may fail, but God is the strength of my heart and my portion forever.
—Psalm 73:25-26

Some may say I am settling for too little, but asking less is not a loss, and readjusting expectations is not a negative. When I was on my feet, big boisterous pleasures provided only fleeting satisfaction. In a wheelchair, satisfaction settles in as I sit under an oak tree on a windy day and delight in the rustle of leaves or sit by a fire and enjoy the soothing strains of a symphony. These smaller, less noisy pleasures are rich because, unlike the fun on my feet, these things yield patience, endurance, and gratitude, all of which fits me further for eternity.

Yieldedness gains you the most here on earth. You enjoy "a sincere heart in full assurance of faith" (Hebrews 10:22). You enjoy a new degree, a new release of energy at every point in your life as the eye of your soul is strengthened and spiritual understanding is quickened. A greater assurance of faith shows you that all things are, indeed, working together for good, and you realize that the smallest of kind deeds done in Christ's name will result in a greater capacity to serve God in glory.

Suffering hurries the heart homeward.

 From your Bible read carefully and slowly Romans 8:25-31. Based on your study, place a check in the box which best describes your feelings.

❑ I still think suffering is a major obstacle to my faith.
❑ I now see suffering in a different perspective.

Suffering hurries the heart homeward.

❑ I'm still thinking about the implications of what you've said. If I agree with you, do I have to give up complaining?

❑ Other?_____

Lesson 3
Suffering Prepares Us to Meet God

*J*ust think. Suppose you had never in your life known physical pain. No sore back, twisted ankle, or decayed molars. What if you never had to use those crutches or that walker? How could you appreciate the scarred hands with which Christ will greet you?

Yes, Jesus will be the only One in heaven who will bear the scars of life on earth, the print of nails in His hands. On His throne, the risen Christ appears "as a Lamb that had been slain." When we touch His scars, God will give us at least a partial answer to the "Why?" questions about our suffering, commenting to us, "Why not?"

If Jesus went through so much suffering to secure for us that which we don't deserve, why did we complain when we endured on earth only a tiny fraction of what He went through on our behalf? But if, instead, we stifled complaints and rejoiced in the privilege of participating in the sufferings of Christ, we will be overjoyed when His glory bursts on the scene. For "we share in his sufferings in order that we may also share in his glory" (Romans 8:17).

 Maybe you didn't know you had signed up to share Christ's sufferings. Read John 17:14 and Matthew 5:11 that appear in the margin. If our perfect Savior endured suffering, why do we feel betrayed when we experience hardships?

_____

_____

In a way, I wish I could take to heaven my old, tattered Everest & Jennings wheelchair. I would point to the empty seat

I have given them your word and the world has hated them, for they are not of the world any more than I am of the world.
—John 17:14

Blessed are you when people insult you, persecute you and falsely say all kinds of evil against you because of me.
—Matthew 5:11

and say, "Lord, for decades I was paralyzed in this chair. But it showed me how paralyzed You must have felt to be nailed to Your Cross. My limitations taught me something about the limitations You endured when You laid aside Your robes of state and put on the indignity of human flesh."

At that point, with my strong and glorified body, I might sit in it, rub the armrests with my hands, look up at Jesus, and add, "The weaker I felt in this chair, the harder I leaned on You. And the harder I leaned, the more I discovered how strong You are. Thank You, Jesus, for learning obedience in Your suffering. You gave me grace to learn obedience in mine."

Not only will I appreciate the scars of Christ, but also the scars of other believers. There I will see men and women that were cut in pieces, burnt in flames, tortured, persecuted, eaten by beasts, and drowned in the seas—all for the love they had for the Lord. What a privilege it will be to stand near their ranks!

Perhaps we would bite our complaining tongues more often if we stopped to picture the scene in heaven. The examples of other suffering saints are meant to inspire us upward on our heavenly journey home. I love reading the biographies of missionaries like Amy Carmichael or J. Hudson Taylor, people who considered it a privilege to bear their sufferings with grace so they might share in Christ's glory.

Examples of suffering saints are meant to inspire us on our heavenly journey home.

Suppose you had never in your life known emotional pain. No stained reputation. No bruised feelings. No pangs of guilt. What if no one had ever offended you deeply? How could you adequately express your gratitude when you approach the Man of Sorrows who was acquainted with grief?

 Name a grief—an emotional pain—you have experienced that helps you understand the emotional pain Jesus bore for us.

_____

If you were never embarrassed or felt ashamed, you could never grasp how much He loved you when He endured the spit from soldiers, the spinelessness of His disciples, the callousness of the crowd, and the jeers from the mob. All for the love of you.

Lastly, suppose you had never in your life known the struggle against sin. He took your shameful sins and made them His. You will be able to say, "Lord, I'm grateful that I felt the pierc-

ing stab of guilt. I can better appreciate how You were wounded by sin on the Cross!"

 What past sin of yours helps you to appreciate Christ's wounds? In the margin write that sin. Take a moment to thank God for His forgiveness.

There's a distinct connection between heaven and this struggle against sin. The apostle John tightened the connection when he wrote in 1 John 3:2-3, "We know that when he appears, we shall be like him, for we shall see him as he is. Everyone who has this hope in him purifies himself."

Rarely do we find believers who, for the sake of heaven, purify themselves. But I want to be one of them, don't you? I want to sweep my conscience clean and jerk open every closet in my heart that hides a skeleton. It's painful to sit this close to self-scrutiny and cut away every sin that entangles. I don't like "gouging out the eye" or "cutting off the hand" any more than you do. But it's what the Lord requires if we are to possess a lively anticipation of seeing Him face-to-face. Everyone who purifies himself has a heavenly hope, and everyone who possesses this hope, purifies himself.[39]

How often do you take inventory—jerking open those closets, sweeping under the furniture of your heart?

❑ every day   ❑ occasionally
❑ weekly   ❑ seldom
❑ once a month   ❑ never

Possibly you don't know where to start in taking regular inventory of your heart. Proverbs 6:16-19 describes seven things God hates. Use the verses to write your own checklist of character traits you want to clean from your heart.

_____

_____

_____

My checklist reads like this. I want to eliminate from my life pride that elevates me above others, all forms of dishonesty,

There are six things the Lord hates, seven that are detestable to him: haughty eyes, a lying tongue, hands that shed innocent blood, a heart that devises wicked schemes, feet that are quick to rush into evil, a false witness who pours out lies and a man who stirs up dissension among brothers.
—Proverbs 6:16-19

anger that lashes out at others, evil desires, haste, and anything that will stand in the way of loving others.

 Now pray through your list. How are you doing on each of the character qualities—at the heart level as well as at the level of surface actions?

I want to be as happy as possible in heaven. Bishop Ryle is on target when he warns, "Heaven is a holy place. Its inhabitants are all holy. Its occupations are all holy. To be really happy in heaven, it stands to reason...our hearts must be somewhat in tune, somewhat ready for it."[40]

Yes, you want to be happy in heaven. You'd like to feel at home with King David and the apostles Paul and John. Then live a life in agreement with the things they spoke about. Could we enthusiastically greet the apostle Paul who said, "Submit to one another out of reverence for Christ" (Ephesians 5:21) if we made it a practice of stepping on others to get ahead?

Could we look forward to hours alone with the apostle John who said, "Whoever lives in love lives in God, and God in him" (1 John 4:16) if in truth we settled for a halfhearted, ho-hum devotion to our Lord Jesus? Would we really feel comfortable with David who said, "I cry out to God Most High, to God, who fulfills His purpose for me" (Psalm 57:2) if we opted to ignore God when troubles came?

How could we be thrilled to meet the Lord face-to-face after clinging on earth to the very sins for which He died? It is impossible to hold onto sinful habits while, at the same time, holding onto the desire to touch the nail-scarred hands of Christ. No one can hope for heaven while consciously clutching onto sins he knows to be offensive.

True, holy living is rugged and demanding, but its heavenly rewards are precious. The entire seventh chapter of Romans assures us holy living will always be a struggle. But think of it as the best way of showing love to Christ! I want to cut away every sin that entangles.

The Suffering That Liberates

A curious thing will happen if you view your suffering as preparation to meet God. You won't be quick to call it "suffering" again. Even though I have rough moments in my wheelchair, for the most part I consider my paralysis a gift. Just as Jesus exchanged the meaning of the Cross from a symbol of torture to one of hope and salvation, He gives me the grace to

Jesus exchanged the meaning of the Cross from a symbol of torture to one of hope and salvation.

*What proof could you
bring of your love and
faithfulness if this life left
you totally unscarred?*

do the same with my chair. If a cross can become a blessing, so can a wheelchair.

When you meet Jesus face-to-face, your loyalty in your hardships will give you something tangible, something concrete to offer Him in return. For what proof could you bring of your love and faithfulness if this life left you totally unscarred?

 Close your study today by thanking God for those circumstances which were sources of complaint but for which you can choose to praise God.

Lesson 4

When Suffering
Seems Insurmountable

Over the phone, I could hear the puffing and wheezing of Lisa's respirator as she labored to speak between breaths. "Joni, I don't … see why God … is putting me through … all this suffering … Why doesn't He just take me home … now?"

I leaned my head against the receiver and wondered, for the thousandth time, what to say. Lisa was a 21-year-old woman who became severely paralyzed as a result of an accident two and a half years earlier. In that time she had been shifted from one hospital to another. The doctors had done all they could, and now they were deliberating over where to send her next. Her parents couldn't take her in. Independent living centers for people her age were overcrowded with long waiting lists. The only option? A nursing home.

I'd had many years in a wheelchair. Lisa, only a few. How could I expect her to grasp the things that had taken me ages to understand? What could I give or say to help?

 What do you think you would say to Lisa? What would you definitely not say? Write in the margin.

"I'm a Christian," Lisa continued, interrupting my thoughts. "Why do I … have to go through all … this?"

I used to ask myself that many times. Okay, I'll accept this connection between hardship and heaven, but what if the hardship is insurmountable? Overwhelming? Unbearable? I'm paralyzed from the shoulders down, but Lisa is paralyzed from the neck down. She can't even breathe on her own. How can one deal with so much frustration and affliction?

Questions such as these lose their academic tone when couched around the struggles of someone like Lisa—wondering how to live, how to view her affliction as meaningful. This young respirator-dependent quadriplegic is thrust out into a no-man's-land, way ahead of the frontline trenches where most of us suffer. She has an arduous road ahead. When hurting people like her give God an inch, He always takes a mile. He wants those who suffer greatly to receive even greater glory.

Great Suffering Can Result in Great Glory

There is a direct relationship between earth's suffering and heaven's glory. I'm not glorifying suffering here. There's no inherent goodness in Lisa's spinal cord injury. There's nothing applaudable about the agony. Problems are real, and I'm not denying that suffering hurts. I'm just denying that it matters in the grander scheme of things. It is light and momentary compared with what our response is producing for us in heaven — yes, suffering is pivotal to future glory. This places Lisa in that enviable position I mentioned earlier.

Let me explain. The greatest suffering that ever occurred happened on the Cross. And the greatest glory ever given in response to suffering was the glory ascribed to Christ when He ascended. He suffered "death on a cross...Therefore God exalted him to the highest place" (Philippians 2:8-9). There is a direct correspondence between suffering and glory.

When the mother of James and John approached the Lord and asked if her sons could please enjoy a position of prominence in the kingdom of heaven, the Lord replied, "You don't know what you're asking." Then He said to her sons, "Can you drink the cup I am going to drink?"

"We can," they answered.

Jesus said to them, "You will indeed drink from my cup" (see Matthew 20:20-23).

The Lord inferred that if His followers were to share in His glory, they would also have to share in His sufferings. And the deeper the suffering, the higher the glory. This is why the apostle Peter could say that to the degree one suffers, keep on rejoicing, "Rejoice that you participate in the sufferings of Christ, so that you may be overjoyed when His glory is revealed" (1 Peter 4:13). We rejoice on earth so that we may be overjoyed in heaven.

We rejoice on earth so that we may be overjoyed in heaven.

I want to know Christ and the power of his resurrection and the fellowship of sharing in his sufferings, becoming like him in his death,
—Philippians 3:10

Pain is mandatory, but growth is optional.

Does this mean that those who suffer greatly, yet nobly, will have a bigger halo? A shinier face? No, but it does mean that they will enjoy a greater capacity to serve God in heaven.

 Read Philippians 3:10. A part of knowing Christ fully involves the fellowship of sharing in His suffering, and fellowship with Christ is as good as it gets.

I'm sure there will be times when Lisa will smirk—like I did—as she reads Romans 8:18, "I consider that our present sufferings are not worth comparing with the glory that will be revealed in us." Like me, she will go through cycles, thinking, Is the Bible being flippant about my lot in life? But as long as she keeps focused on the basics—being still and knowing God through prayer and Scripture—she will remain on the high road home. Much depends on the attitude I choose toward my suffering. Often the pain is mandatory, but the growth is optional.

 Choose the best summary statement of the thought in the paragraph above.

- ❑ Suffering isn't really painful; the Bible teaches me to make light of suffering.
- ❑ If I concentrate on knowing God, suffering can help me to value His kingdom.
- ❑ Suffering is always beneficial, no matter how I choose to respond to it.

 Suffering is not automatically redemptive. Below describe what you need to do to grow through suffering.

_____

_____

When the Passage Is Painful
It may be brighter at twilight, but not necessarily easier. For many, the final passage is ugly and painful.

It was this way for Billie Barrows, the wife of Cliff Barrows. For more than 40 years they labored together with Dr. Graham, full of zest for life and zeal for the good fight. That zeal buoyed Billie during her last nine years as she wrestled courageously against breast cancer, which spread into her liver, bones, and finally, her brain. She chose the high road and kept a joyful outlook, building up her body with the medicine of a happy heart. But even with five chemotherapy treatments, Billie could not stave off the disease.

Surrounded by a loving family, boosted by prayer, and bolstered by a fighting spirit, hers should have been the model passage—wonderfully serene with chariots swinging low as the angels quietly came to carry her home. It wasn't that way. It was a knock-down-drag-out fight in the center ring, with time bullying and battering and showing no mercy.

On five different occasions her sons and daughters flew from the far corners of the country to join their dad at Billie's bedside. Surely this time God will take Mother home, they reasoned. But it was not her appointed time. During the last two weeks Billie's joy, which had been such an inspiration to Cliff, friends, doctors, and the family was silenced by the ticking of each painful minute that failed to bring release.

The deathbed was not a place of blessing for Billie. But it did become a place of blessing for the family. Cliff and his sons and daughters, in-laws, and grandchildren discovered a deeper, richer blessing in being together around a bed of affliction that poignantly offered moments of love and reconciliation. Although Billie couldn't communicate, the large tears that rolled down her cheeks right before she died, said it all. Finally, blessed release came. She left the land of the dying for the land of the living.

Not long after Billie's funeral, I called her daughter, Bonnie. We talked about the wrenching agony of those last days. "Joni, Christians shouldn't glamorize death. Death is Satan's last-ditch effort, and he's going to make it as awful as he can."

There was a long pause. "But God has the last word. Resurrection. And at the graveside we were able to sing—actually, we kept singing it every day—

Soar we now where Christ has led,
Following our exalted Head,
Made like Him, like Him we rise,
Ours the cross, the grave, the skies."

I could hear the smile in Bonnie's voice, and it wasn't hard to imagine that same smile through tears as she and her family left the graveside singing that hymn of victory, "Christ the Lord Has Risen Today."

Death is Satan's last-ditch effort, but God has the last word.

 In the margin, explain how Jesus' resurrection affects your attitude about death? about the death of your loved ones?

As I hung up, I thought of Corrie ten Boom, the Dutch woman who was sent to a Nazi concentration camp for hiding Jewish families. Years after Tante Corrie's release, her companion, Pam Rosewell, sat by her bedside when she was old and stroke-stricken. Watching Corrie's mind and body waste away to a thin shadow of her former self, she wondered — much like Billie's family — why the Lord didn't take Tante Corrie home sooner. Pam observed after the funeral of her elderly friend, "Every day she lived was a victory over the devil ... he would have had her die 50 years earlier in Ravensbruck, but just the act of living, without doing a thing, just breathing life in and out was a triumph. If her final years had not influenced any person on earth and if the only reason the Lord allowed her to remain on earth was to make a silent daily statement to the principalities in heavenly places that 'Jesus is victor,' then it was an important silence indeed."

In all their suffering, neither Corrie nor Billie were diminished.

 Think about the statement: "You can tell a lot about a person's life by the way he or she dies."

Lesson 5

Heaven Is Your Strength

The firmer my heart becomes anchored in heaven, the more I want to go there. Now.

*L*isa will have to go through another cycle. I still deal with it and I bet you do too. The firmer my heart becomes anchored in heaven, the more I want to go there. Now.

It has nothing to do with being tired of sitting down or getting cricks in my neck from holding up my head all day. It's just that less of my heart is here, and more of it is there. I identify with the apostle Paul who said in Philippians 1:21, "For me, to live is Christ, and to die is gain. If I am to go on living in the body, this will mean fruitful labor for me. Yet what shall I choose? I don't know! I am torn between the two: I desire to depart and be with Christ, which is better by far; but it is more necessary for you that I remain in the body."

How much of your desire is like Paul's, "to depart and be with Christ"? How much to continue "fruitful living"? Place a dot below to express your desire.

I want to continue fruitful living.	I want to be with Christ.

Like Paul, I often debate the pros and cons of life. Like him, my earthly life is meant to be one of discontentment. I am torn between the two. I desire to depart. Since my heart has already gone ahead, I long to follow it home. But it is more necessary that I—Lisa, and thousands like us—remain in the body. For others.

 Who are some of the "others" you need to serve while you remain on earth? Name at least three persons or ministries God has called you to.

_____

_____

_____

At the close of my phone conversation with Lisa I said, "If you remain faithful, despite the odds, it helps people like me more than you'll ever know."

"But it's hard ... to think of others ... when you're hurting."

"I know. But it is more necessary for you to remain in the body ... it is more necessary for me and many more who know you better. A fellow with a disability once wrote, 'For just as the sufferings of Christ flow over into our lives, so also through Christ our comfort overflows. If we are distressed, it is for your comfort and salvation; if we are comforted, it is for your comfort, which produces in you patient endurance of the same sufferings we suffer'" (2 Corinthians 1:5-6).

There was a long pause at the other end.

"The fact that you hang in there ... does something for the rest of us Christians. I'm not talking about your being an inspiration. It's more than that ... it's a mystery. God somehow strengthens others by your faithfulness. You may feel like a burden to others, but God thinks the opposite. He thinks it's necessary that others take care of you. You will be doing more for their spiritual well-being than you can imagine."

God somehow strengthens others by your faithfulness.

129

> *It is more necessary for you that I remain in the body. Convinced of this, I know that I will remain, and I will continue with all of you for your progress and joy in the faith, so that through my being with you again your joy in Christ Jesus will overflow on account of me.*
> —Philippians 1:24-26

 According to Philippians 1:24-26, what would Paul's continued presence with them do for his fellow believers?

_____

_____

 Does your presence cause fellow believers to overflow with joy in Christ Jesus? How can you be a more faithful witness to the joy found in fellowship with Christ?

_____

_____

Lisa and I continued to keep in touch. She settled into a living situation with a friend and began to attend a local college. She got involved with her church and started going to Bible study. After five years, we lost contact. I wasn't worried about her, though, because she seemed to be on a steady path.

This year, however, I got the shock of my life when, after I finished speaking at a conference, a young woman hooked up to a ventilator wheeled up to me with a confident smile. I knew immediately who she was. The light in her eyes assured me this was the same young woman. She was happily heading for home and making the most of every day on the way.

Lisa and I have seen the future, a glorious future for those who, for Christ's sake, suffer valiantly.

Onward and Upward

Suffering always drives us in deeper and up higher. Always onward and upward into the heart of heaven. Then, rest.

Not the rest of inactivity but rest from pain, weariness, and disappointment. Like many who have toiled for years, I'm ready for rest. No more wrestling against sin. No more prying the world's suction cups off my heart. No knock-down-drag-out fights with the devil. No collapsing in bed after an exhausting day only to snatch a few hours before you are up again.

This thought alone makes the earthly toil not only bearable, but lighter. I can remember how, after hours of riding my horse, my weary mount would be wet with sweat, her head hanging low. I had to urge her to put one tired hoof in front of another. Then as soon as she caught a whiff of home or recognized the fences of her own pasture, her ears would pick up and her pace would quicken. The nearer we came to the barn, the more eager her trot. After a quick unsaddling, she would joyfully roll in the dirt and take long deep drinks from the trough. How good it feels for a beast to be home, to be able to rest.

How good it will feel for us to rest, to be at home.

Maybe the writers of the Bible had this sweet rest in mind, a rest that perked them up and quickened their pace. They wrote vigorous encouragements like, "Let us, therefore, make every effort to enter that rest" and "Seeing that the days are short, make every effort" and "Redeem the time for the days are evil." The weary labor for them seemed featherweight compared with the glorious rest they were about to enter.

God has placed suffering in your life to remind you that heaven is not only for the future; it is for now, for this present moment. Heaven is meant to bless your path and be a source of strength in your suffering today. Valiantly welcome and greet it.

Heaven is not only for the future; it is for now, for this present moment.

Review the lessons you have completed this week. Write at least three things you have discovered about heaven (or maybe ideas you have discovered to be false about heaven).

_____

_____

_____

In what way has this week's study changed your passion for heaven?

_____

_____

Write a prayer expressing your feelings to God about your work this week.

_____

_____

_____

Unit 7

How Do I Get
Ready for Heaven?

*W*hy am I always surprised at how fast sunsets disappear? How fast my days disappear?

My life will be gone in a flash, in the twinkling of an eye. Suddenly—just like that—it will be over. Finished. The fading beauty of all the good things in life will disappear.

Drink it all in. This life won't last forever. Sooner than I realize, I will follow that sunset over the horizon and step into the other side of eternity. If I'm able to look over my shoulder at earth, I know I'll be stunned that life went by so rapidly. But in heaven, there will literally be no time to think about it.

So I must think about it now.

That's why God gives us timeless moments in the here and now, striking that resonant chord in our heart that echoes eternity. He woos us away from this world with that heavenly haunting when we're enfolded in the arms of the one we love, or watch a baby break into a giggle, or savor a Scripture that springs to life in our hearts.

Timeless moments are those that send our hearts on ahead to heaven. Moments when we demonstrate drastic obedience, choose patience over complaint, or honor God when it's hard.

"Be very careful, then, how you live—not as unwise but as wise, making the most of every opportunity, because the days are evil," Ephesians 5:15 echoes. Days are fleeting, hours are fading. Before you know it, we will no longer have the chance to prove our love to Jesus with our obedience. We won't have time to get back on track, to build with gold, silver, and precious stones.

The sun will have set.

What You'll Learn in This Unit

This week you will look toward the true glory of heaven—Jesus. He is the Bridegroom who comes for His bride. He brings joy and a great banquet, but He also brings the great and terrible day of the Lord.

Unit Scripture

Surely this is our God; we trusted in him, and he saved us. This is the Lord, we trusted in him; let us rejoice and be glad in his salvation. —Isaiah 25:9

Lesson 1

Waiting on the Groom

We may be separated from our Savior, but that's no reason to sit around killing time until He comes. Jesus explains what brides ought to be doing while they're waiting for their grooms:

> At that time the kingdom of heaven will be like ten virgins who took their lamps and went out to meet the bridegroom. Five of them were foolish and five were wise. The foolish ones took their lamps but did not take any oil with them. The wise, however, took oil in jars along with their lamps. The bridegroom was a long time in coming, and they all became drowsy and fell asleep.
>
> At midnight the cry rang out: "Here's the bridegroom! Come out to meet him!"
>
> Then all the virgins woke up and trimmed their lamps. The foolish ones said to the wise, "Give us some of your oil; our lamps are going out."
>
> "No," they replied, "there may not be enough for both us and you. Instead, go to those who sell oil and buy some for yourselves."
>
> But while they were on their way to buy the oil, the bridegroom arrived. The virgins who were ready went in with him to the wedding banquet. And the door was shut. Later the others also came. "Sir! Sir!" they said. "Open the door for us!"
>
> But he replied, "I tell you the truth, I don't know you."
>
> Therefore keep watch, because you do not know the day or the hour" (Matthew 25:1-13).

 Write in one sentence what Jesus was teaching with the parable of the 10 virgins.

_____

_____

Foolish virgins think that the betrothal is just one big insurance policy guaranteeing them access to the wedding without

Foolish virgins think the betrothal is just one big insurance policy.

Wait for the Lord; be strong and take heart and wait for the Lord.
—Psalm 27:14

lifting a finger. Wise virgins understand the betrothal carries with it big responsibilities. They recognize they are married, albeit separated from the groom, so they watch. They work. They stay awake. They pour their hearts into the marriage covenant. In short, they act like they are loved and in love.

 Psalm 27:14 is only one of many Scriptures urging us to wait for the Lord. Check each of the following that you believe are part of waiting for the Lord.

- ❑ Sell everything and move to a mountaintop.
- ❑ Love Him with a passion.
- ☒ Live in expectation of Jesus' return.
- ❑ Seek to tell everyone the good news of salvation.
- ❑ Sit around and wait.
- ❑ Figure out when He will return.

Before you rush to assume that waiting means doing something, remember it means being someone. To wait is an occupation of the heart. To wait on the Lord is to love Him with spirited affection and passionate delight. To wait on Him is to fix your eyes on those converging points in eternity: Jesus.

The Bridegroom invites us to know Him intimately. Jesus presses home the point about this intimacy more dramatically in John 6:53-57. Read these verses in the margin.

No wonder language like that sent the disciples scattering! But remember, He's talking about a spiritual intimacy. Thankfully, my wheelchair helps with spiritual intimacy. I get exhausted after a long day of sitting, and so most evenings I have to lie down around 7:30. Lying in bed paralyzed, I have all the time in the world to wait on Jesus, to focus the eyes of my heart on those heavenly coordinates.

Lying there, looking at the ceiling, I squint my eyes of faith to focus on unseen divine realities and their future fulfillments. I set my heart and mind on heavenly glories above.

I tell you the truth, unless you eat the flesh of the Son of Man and drink his blood, you have no life in you. ... For my flesh is real food and my blood is real drink. Whoever eats my flesh and drinks my blood remains in me, and I in him. Just as the living Father sent me and I live because of the Father, so the one who feeds on me will live because of me.
—John 6:53-57

Can you identify a time and place when you made the decision to "set your heart and mind on heavenly glories"? ❑ Yes ❑ No If so, be prepared to share your story with your group.

In the face-to-face intimacy I enjoy with my betrothed, I take Him at His word and "eat the flesh of the Son of Man and drink his blood."

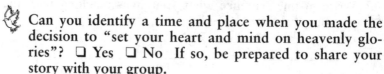

Feeding on Him? I "taste and see that the Lord is good" (Psalm 34:8) as I ingest favorite Scriptures.

Drinking His blood? "[His] love is more delightful than wine" (Song of Songs 1:2) in praying and singing hymns.

When I meditate on Him, I'm in the heavenlies, picturing myself kneeling in the throne room where Jesus is seated. Maybe one evening I'll imagine I'm His handmaiden serving at the foot of His throne. Another evening, I'm His fellow intercessor kneeling next to Him in the Garden of Gethsemane. On another night, His sister or His child. If I'm under spiritual attack, I go to Him as the Captain of the heavenly hosts.

 Review the paragraph you just read. In the margin list different roles Jesus plays in our lives.

 As you build your relationship with Jesus, which of the roles do you most need to claim personally?

This intimate spiritual union is a two-way street. Occasionally, I'll picture Jesus whispering something to me that the Father said to Him in Isaiah 42:1: "Here is my servant, whom I uphold, my chosen one in whom I delight." Jesus wants us to love Him passionately and single-heartedly, but He more than matches it with love, pure and fervent.

On some evenings, He's the father running down the trail to embrace me, the prodigal, before I can speak a word of contrition. At other times, He is the farmer showering on me a full day's wage when I've hardly worked. On other evenings, He is the master forgiving me, the sinful woman, before I realize I've done anything wrong. He's the king lavishing on me a banquet when I'm not even aware I'm malnourished.[41]

Intimate spiritual union is a two-way street.

 Number the following roles 1 to 4 according to which best describes how you have experienced God's love.

  _2_ the father running to meet me—His prodigal child
  ___ the farmer paying a generous wage
  _1_ the master forgiving my sin
  ___ the king lavishing on me a banquet I do not deserve

 Talk honestly with God. Share your gratitude with Him about these roles He plays in your life.

This is eternal life: that they may know you, the only true God, and Jesus Christ, whom you have sent."
—*John 17:3*

The surpassing greatness of knowing Christ Jesus my Lord, for whose sake I have lost all things. I consider them rubbish, that I may gain Christ and be found in him, not having a righteousness of my own that comes from the law, but that which is through faith in Christ— the righteousness that comes from God and is by faith."
—*Philippians 3:8-9*

While the Groom Is Absent

Knowing Jesus this way is "heaven." I mean that literally. Eternal life is knowledge of God. When we deepen our relationship with Jesus, we get a head start on our eternal life right here on earth. Heaven is already happening to us.

 Remember our physics discussion about heaven as the fifth dimension? How far away is heaven (page 21)?

Two kinds of knowledge of Jesus exist. Just ask the wise and foolish virgins. If you asked a foolish virgin, "Do you know Jesus?" she would probably say, "Yes, I gave my heart to Him at a retreat in 1962, so I'm saved and going to heaven." She's reading a statement right off her insurance policy.

What would the wise virgin reply? "Yes, I know Jesus. I've given my life to Him, and I enjoy such wonderful intimacy with Him in prayer and studying His Word. Let me tell you about some of the experiences we've shared together. Honestly, spending time with Him is the highlight of my day."

The apostle Paul wrote in Philippians 3:8-9 of his position with God. It's wonderful to have this kind of right standing (that's what righteousness means), but there's more to knowing Christ. There's the bride/bridegroom thing. It's a different kind of knowledge. Paul touches on this deeper knowledge in the next verses when he yearns, "I want to know Christ and the power of his resurrection and the fellowship of sharing in his sufferings, becoming like him in his death, and so, somehow, to attain to the resurrection from the dead" (Philippians 3:10-11).

God covers His end of the relationship when He positions us in Christ. Positioning is His responsibility. We cover our end of the relationship on earth as we experience the depths of knowing God. Experiencing is our responsibility in fitting ourselves for heaven. It's what wise virgins do while they wait.

 That was too important to miss. As a review, after the following list of responsibilities, write either "mine" or "His":

To position me in Christ _____
To experience the depths of knowing God _____
To develop my love relationship with God _mine_

Right now, the bridegroom is absent. But, oh, I can hardly wait for the day when I break through to see the face of Jesus and once and for all know Him. Time will stand still in a heavenly ecstasy!

 Is your heart beginning to be hungrier for God? Do you desire for your "thirst" for Him to grow? Go for a walk with Him. Take along your book, and reminisce about what growth you have experienced and what joys you have shared as you have studied your real home.

Lesson 2

The Wedding Gift

It's common practice for newlyweds to give gifts to each other. I suppose when I finally see my Savior, my gift to Him shall be whatever bits and pieces of earthly obedience I've done as evidence of my love. He said, "If anyone loves me, he will obey my teaching" (John 14:23), and I'm sure these bits and pieces will sparkle and shine like diamonds.

But what shall He give to us?

He will give the joy of heaven. Isaiah 35:10 is a peek at the gift. To have my head crowned with everlasting joy is one of those earthly images that looks askew, but I don't mind. People caught up in ecstasy don't worry about such things. Suffice to say, it's a gift. A crowning gift.

We all think we know what joy is … until we are asked to define it. Go ahead. Give it a try.

_____

_____

Look at the gift with me for a moment. Joy is a fruit of the Spirit. It has in it the essence of eternity. When joy grips us, it always appears new, like a surprise, yet it seems ancient, as though it had always been there. Joy always has in it a timeless, eternal element. Pleasure and happiness may come and go, but joy seems to remain. Happy feelings have nothing of that air of eternity about them that joy has. Joy, in its essence, is of God. He is "the Lord of joy."

As the deer pants for streams of water, so my soul pants for you, O God. My soul thirsts for God, for the living God. When can I go and meet with God?
—Psalm 42:1-2

They will enter Zion with singing; everlasting joy will crown their heads. Gladness and joy will overtake them, and sorrow and sighing will flee away.
—Isaiah 35:10

Joy floods back to God in gratitude, out to others like a fountain, and through our own hearts in a torrent.

Joy is dynamic. It cannot stay stagnant or bottled up. Joy flows. Actually, it overflows. It floods back to God in gratitude, out to others like a fountain, and rushes through our own hearts in a torrent. This is why people weep for joy. We human beings, all finite and compacted, cannot contain the overflow. We are too small for how big joy is, and so we must weep. Joy breaks our hearts, for like love, joy cannot be contained. Remember when I said that lovers find themselves enveloped by something gloriously larger than themselves? Joy is the same. It will *overtake* us, Isaiah 35:10 says. This will be heavenly ecstasy.[42]

As an artist, I see something else about joy. It happens whenever I look at a certain painting that hangs on the office wall opposite my desk. It is a rendering of Mary, the mother of Jesus, and Gabriel, the angel. Whenever my mind is at rest and my desk is clear of work, I find myself drawn into that painting. I lose myself in it.

This experience may happen to you, if not with a painting, then with a great symphony. You're sitting in the symphony hall, your eyes closed, the music swells and surrounds you, and before you know it, you are lost. You have become one with the sounds of the orchestra. Or if you're a left-brained person who isn't into art or music, how about that exhilarating moment when, during the 1982 Winter Olympics, the U.S. hockey team pulverized the Russians? Whether in front of the television, in the stands, or on the ice, we all became "one" in the euphoria of victory.

 What type of event or experience brings you those moments of euphoric joy?

- ❏ art
- ❏ music
- ❏ children
- ❏ other _____
- ❏ sports
- ❏ nature
- ❏ drama

If you have experienced any of this, it's an inkling of the joy that will overtake us when we take just one glance at the Lord of joy. We will lose ourselves in Him. We will become one with Him. We will be "in Christ," we will have "put on Christ" at the deepest, most profound and exhilarating level. The Lord's wedding gift to us will be the joy of sharing totally in His nature without us losing our identity. Thanks be to God for His indescribable gift!

Heaven is more than just a place of pleasure and happiness. If that were so, heaven would be boring. Pleasure is always seeking satisfaction. Happiness is finding satisfaction. But whether reached through pleasure or happiness, there is still something inert about satisfaction. It's a little too "still." That's why joy is satisfaction that is always moving. It bursts beyond pleasure and happiness; it calls for rejoicing out of sheer generosity. It is the real energy of praise. If we are to be praising God for all of eternity, which we shall be, then joy will be the dynamic.

Joy is the real energy of praise.

One night, during the evening ice cream social at another one of our JAF Ministries' family retreats, I powered my chair over to little red-haired Nicole in her wheelchair; Tiffany, her friend; and Rachel, standing next to her in her leg braces. After a couple of comments about the ice cream, we were soon playing a game of tag. Wheelchair tag. Before long, a kid in a walker joined us, along with his sister, a child with Down syndrome, and her brother. Weaving in and out around the legs of the adults, we giggled and screamed as our foot pedals clunked together, bumping and bouncing like Dodge'm cars.

After the ice cream began to melt, John, our retreat director, looked at his watch and tried to herd the families back to their cabins. But we were so caught up in the game that I lost all track of time. Only after we waved goodnight did I realize it was like heaven. It was heaven because of the play and the joy and the sense of timelessness. Right before I entered my cabin, I looked up to the stars and thanked Jesus for the sneak preview of heaven's joy. I had to smile at His answer from Matthew 19:14: "Let the little children come to me ... for the kingdom of heaven belongs to such as these."

As I lay in bed that night, the entire experience of joyful play kept echoing. The kingdom of heaven belongs to giggling, happy, carefree children. I kept thinking and straining my ears—or was I trying to open the eyes of my heart—to hear or see more. I knew there was much more than just play in that experience. I had touched a moment of great happiness and wisdom. I didn't realize it then, but I had touched eternity in time. Months later I came across another quote by Peter Kreeft that nailed it:

> *When we touch eternity in time, it's like an echo. We smell the salt air of the sea, even here, far upstream in the river of time. Whenever we touch wisdom or love, we swim in salt water. Earth is God's beach and when we are*

wise and loving, we are infants splashing happily in the wavelets of 'that immortal sea.' But when we are spiritually full grown, we will buoyantly plow its breakers of wisdom and be borne up by its bottomless depths of love. Boredom, like pain, will be remembered only as a joke when we are drenched in joy.[43]

 We began this lesson with a most daunting task—to understand the essence of joy. Look back to your starting definition on page 137. Below write how you would change that definition after studying this lesson.

_____

_____

 Thank God for the sheer, overwhelming, unbridled joy of heaven and for the little tastes of it we get here on earth.

Lesson 3

The Bridegroom Cometh!

And so now, we wait. We wait for our bridegroom. "I wait for the Lord, my soul waits, and in his word I put my hope. My soul waits for the Lord more than watchmen wait for the morning" (Psalm 130:5-6). We lean on the windowsill of eternity, look to the sky, and whisper, "Come quickly, Lord Jesus, come quickly."

Oh, when will He come?

Have you ever been so deeply in love that it hurt to be separated from your beloved—even for a little while? Does our Bridegroom deserve such love?

Every once in a while, when our heart grows weary of waiting, the Lord revives us with snatches of joy, such as the kind I experienced at that retreat. Earthly joy is a preview of the joy that will overtake us when, finally, our Lord returns.

And it will all happen in the twinkling of an eye. Before we realize it, if we are blessed to be living at the time of His return,

The Lord himself will come down from heaven, with a loud command, with the voice of the archangel and with the trumpet call of God, and the dead in Christ will rise first. After that, we who are still alive and are left will be caught up together with them in the clouds to meet the Lord in the air. And so we will be with the Lord forever."
—*1 Thessalonians 4:16-17*

we shall find ourselves in the embrace of our Savior at the wedding supper of the Lamb. Heaven will have arrived. The Lord's overcoming of the world will be a lifting of the curtain of our five senses, and we shall see the whole universe in plain sight. Life and immortality will no longer be dim thoughts, but vivid and strikingly real. At first, the shock of joy may burn with the brilliant newness of being glorified, but in the next instant we will be at peace and feel at home, as though it were always this way, that we were born for such a place. At that moment, earth will seem like a half-forgotten dream, pleasant enough, but only a dream.[44]

I imagine great multitudes of people rushing from jungles of roses, down banks of violets, pulsing with light and songs of birds and the voices of angels.

"Are all here?" someone will shout.

A voice will echo, "Yes, we are all here!"

 Now, enjoy an unseen divine reality. Picture yourself taking a seat at heaven's wedding supper. Describe what you see. Then read my description below.

Open the eyes of your heart and marvel at the crystal-clear glory, the dazzle of light, a holy city, the New Jerusalem sparkling like a prism. Picture a banquet hall resplendent with banners, stunning with jewels and joy-filled music. The celebration will kick off with a loud and resounding "Hallelujah! For our Lord God Almighty reigns. Let us rejoice and be glad and give him glory! For the wedding of the Lamb has come, and his bride has made herself ready" (Revelation 19:6-7).

As you pull up a chair to the banquet table, take a look at what's on the menu from Isaiah 25:6-8: "On this mountain the Lord Almighty will prepare a feast of rich food for all peoples, a banquet of aged wine—the best of meats and the finest of wines. On this mountain he will destroy the shroud that enfolds all peoples, the sheet that covers all nations; he will swallow up death forever. The Sovereign Lord will wipe away the tears from all faces; he will remove the disgrace of his people from all the earth. The Lord has spoken."

There's no mistaking. This is a real banquet. And a specific one too. I get a charge just thinking about it! I wonder who will sit next to me, or across from me. I glance down the table and there's my friend, Verna Estes, mother of seven, swapping baby stories with Susanna Wesley, mother of 17. There's her pastor-husband, Steve, getting the lowdown on Romans 6 from

There's no mistaking. This is a real banquet.

141

the apostle Paul. There's Moses toasting Martin Luther. Billy Graham talking with a junior-high Sunday School teacher. My husband Ken (whose lifelong ambition was to fly an F-14 fighter) cornering astronaut James Irwin.

At the other end of the table, Fanny Crosby is doing harmony on one of her hymns with the widow who faithfully played the rickety piano at the nursing home every Sunday. As for me, as soon as I see my friends who spent years getting me up in the mornings—Carolyn, Francie, Judy, Jay, Bev, and Irene—I jump up and grab a platter of meat. I can't wait to serve them something.

 Think of the faces around that banquet table. Who do you most want to serve?

_____

Who do you most long to see?

_____

Who do you most want to meet there?

_____

Then I'll look up and walking toward me will be Dad and Mother. He'll give me his ol' thumbs-up and a wink, my mother will start giggling, and before you know it, we'll break up into uncontrollable laughter. We will try to stop, then break up again, laughing and pointing at everybody. "Look at this! Can you believe we're here! I knew it was true, but not this true!"

Since we always sang together as a family on earth, I'm sure we'll break into song right there around the table.

 Time out! I know the songs of heaven will eclipse any song of earth, but name three songs you love that you can look forward to singing there—with perfect pitch and a range you only imagined here.

1. _____

2. _____

3. _____

Now stop the music. Stop the moving picture and let's retrace an earlier question. Will there be plates, knives, and forks at the wedding banquet? Will someone be back in the kitchen shuffling pots and pans to cook stuff in? Will there be mixers and trash compactors? And what about the meat? Certainly there won't be slaughterhouses in heaven! Will Arabs eat with their fingers? Will Asians use chopsticks? Will people in hell do cleanup duty?

These questions seem ridiculous now. In light of the glorious celebration, who cares? I'm sure it'll be made plain. All I care about is that it is real.

A real streamers-and-confetti celebration that death has died.

A real ticker-tape parade announcing victory over sin.

The whole earth will join in the party, and "you will go out in joy and be led forth in peace; the mountains and hills will burst into song before you, and all the trees of the field will clap their hands" (Isaiah 55:12). Christ will open our eyes to the great fountain of love in His heart for us, beyond all that we ever saw before. It will hit us that we, the church, are His bride. Not just individually, but together. United. One with each other, and one with Him. Suddenly, our joy is multiplied a millionfold.

Then, we will join hands around the banquet table, and "in that day [we] will say, 'Surely this is our God; we trusted in him, and he saved us. This is the Lord, we trusted in him; let us rejoice and be glad in his salvation' " (Isaiah 25:9).

And the party is just beginning!

 End your lesson with a song of praise. Yes, you can sing it in the shower if you like, just so you sing it to Jesus. May I suggest verses 2 and 4 of a familiar hymn, "My Jesus I Love Thee:"

I love thee because thou has first loved me,
And purchased my pardon on Calvary's tree;
I love thee for wearing the thorns on thy brow;
If ever I loved Thee, my Jesus, 'tis now.

In mansions of glory and endless delight,
I'll ever adore Thee in heaven so bright;
And singing Thy praises, before Thee I'll bow.
If ever I loved Thee, my Jesus, 'tis now.[45]

Lesson 4
Winning Through Weakness

On earth, Jesus never acted like a king. Or at least not like one would think a king should act. Jesus, however, had a good reason for cloaking His majesty under the robe of weakness, shame, and humility. When the Father designed the plan of salvation, He initiated a scheme that would ultimately bring the highest and brightest glory to His Son, the King of the Cosmos. It was a plot that almost reads like an adventure story.

Now any struggle between a hero and the bad guys is interesting enough, but when the hero is disadvantaged, a new element is introduced. Now the hero is in far more danger and he appears to have less chance of winning. But if in his weakness he overcomes against all odds, he ends up twice as much the hero. When weak heroes outmaneuver strong villains, the victory is awe-inspiring.

So, the Prince of Peace, the Lamb who let Himself be slain, will be glorified, not because He employed brute force against Satan, but because He didn't.

The Lamb who let Himself be slain will be glorified.

 Draw on what you've read about Jesus in your Bible. Name at least three ways our Lord allowed Himself to be weak or disadvantaged. (Here are some hints. Check Isaiah 53:2-7; Philippians 2:6-8; 2 Corinthians 13:4; and Hebrews 2:9.)

_____

_____

_____

The King Who Won Against All Odds

There's another aspect of the Father's plan which positions His Son as less than kingly, yet guarantees Him greater glory. It involves defeating the strong villain by using his own dark power against him.

It's kind of like judo.

My husband Ken could tell you all about it. Every once in a while he gets into his martial arts mode and starts jumping around the living room like a cat on catnip, pouncing helter-skelter, punching the air with his fists, and kicking toward the ceiling with the side of his foot. I always watch with distracted feminine interest.

Ken tells me that judo has its uses. It's the art of using the power of your enemy to defeat him; and although Ken may appear passive and even weak in a judo match, the secret is simply to wait for that moment when the opponent's full strength can be used to defeat him. When my husband is attacked, he simply judos his assailant and sends the guy flying over his shoulder.

Jesus appeared passive and weak. People kept looking for His crown. We kept hoping He would behave as a monarch should and make the lives of His subjects happy, healthy, and free from trouble. But Jesus had other plans for earth—plans that involved greater praise for the believer and glory for Himself.

He kept doing judo. Especially against the devil. And most specifically at the cross. At the exact moment the devil thought he had Christ cornered and pinned down in defeat, Satan unleashed his full fury to finish Him off. But it was Christ's weakness and vulnerability that enabled Him to judo Satan into slitting his own throat.

Has God ever used "divine judo" for your good, maybe when you didn't understand or desire it? Sometimes the darkest moments in our lives turn out to be the time when God wins a victory we cannot begin to understand until much later.

James Stewart, the Scottish theologian, put it this way:

The very triumphs of His foes He used for their defeat. He compelled their dark achievements to subserve His ends, not theirs. They nailed Him to the tree, not knowing that by that very act they were bringing the world to His feet. They gave Him a cross, not guessing that He would make it a throne.

They flung Him outside the gates to die, not knowing that at that very moment they were lifting up all the gates of the universe to let the King of Glory come in. They thought to root out His doctrines, not understanding that they were implanting imperishably in the hearts of men the very name they intended to destroy.

> *The secret is to wait for that moment when the opponent's full strength can be used to defeat him.*

They thought they had God with His back to the wall, pinned and helpless and defeated. They did not know it was God Himself who had dragged them down to that point. He did not conquer in spite of the dark mystery of evil, He conquered through it.[46]

Something glorious happened when the cross, a symbol of torture, became a symbol of life and hope.

Something glorious happened when the world's worst murder became the world's only salvation. When the cross, a symbol of torture, became a symbol of life and hope, it meant triple the glory.

Jesus ends up triple the hero in heaven because He won using weapons of warfare that were spiritual, not carnal. His triumph was assured using divine judo. He won using perfect timing and patience. "At just the right time, when we were still powerless, Christ died for the ungodly" (Romans 5:6). He won through waiting, yielding, and submission.

Philippians 2:7-9 reads like "The Basic Principles in Martial Arts" because the weaker Christ became, the greater was His victory, and the greater the victory, the more glorious the honors: "[He] made himself nothing. ... He humbled himself and became obedient to death—even death on a cross! Therefore God exalted him to the highest place and gave him the name that is above every name."

If we pitied Christ on earth or felt badly that His justice seemed aborted, we wasted our time. If we were embarrassed for His sake over so much senseless suffering, we would have done better to take a few lessons in the martial arts. Jesus did flex His muscles as King on earth; our unskilled eyes, hearts, and minds just weren't trained to see it. He wore a crown; it just wasn't the crown we expected. Not one of gold, but of thorns.

Up in heaven, we may be tempted to smack our foreheads and exclaim, "Oh bother! How did we miss it?" But there will be no room for remorse. We won't berate ourselves for not having seen it. No, our King of kings will be too gracious to permit us such regrets.

His medals of monarchy were hidden to help us exercise faith, develop trust, and demonstrate obedience, as well as to teach us timing and patience, waiting and yielding. The King overcame the cross so that we might have power to parlay a bullying devil and thus accept our thorns, share our burdens, and carry our own crosses, while all the time turning tragedy into triumph and heartaches into victories.

How does the assurance in Hebrews 2:10 that Jesus became perfect through suffering affect your attitude about your own thorns, burdens, and crosses?

With good grace, Jesus will not scold us for being so us-centered. He will assure us He knew our frame and remembered that we were but dust. We will realize that on earth we were worse than we thought, but the Lord's grace went deeper than we thought, and so in heaven we will do better than we thought.[47]

The Lord Jesus will be exuberant with His kindness, letting it spill and splash over everything. Even our regrets. And that, dear friends, will compel us to love, praise, and rejoice in Him all the more. At that point, God's glory in heaven will open up exponentially to the hundredth power.

I get so happy for Jesus when I picture this moment, for He will show Himself as He is, no longer the weak and suffering servant, but the mighty Sovereign of time and space. His reputation will be vindicated. He will receive all the credit due Him, plus triple the glory. Most of all, His justice will be served.

And it won't look very nice. At least to some.

Close your study today by following the command of Revelation 14:7—fear God and give Him glory. Give Him glory for creating everything that is. Give Him glory for emptying Himself and becoming a man. And give Him glory for conquering every power in the universe.

In bringing many sons to glory, it was fitting that God, for whom and through whom everything exists, should make the author of their salvation perfect through suffering.
—Hebrews 2:10

He said in a loud voice, "Fear God and give him glory, because the hour of his judgment has come. Worship him who made the heavens, the earth, the sea and the springs of water."
—Revelation 14:7

Lesson 5

The Great and Terrible Day of the Lord

*A*ll this stuff about weakness and humility grates on the nerves of some people. They don't buy a God who would let Himself be mocked, kicked, and spit upon, all for the sake of justice, especially justice on their behalf. How dare this weak, powerless God assert that they need to be saved—and from their sin, no less!

On earth, they pushed their own kind of justice. First on their agenda was to defame and defrock Jesus. Setting themselves up at the center of their own moral universe, they thought they had the power to put God on trial. They accused and banished Him as some impotent third-rate deity. Profaning His name, they neutered God and tamed Him so He would bless their lusts and passions.

But in heaven, the record will be set straight. God will vindicate His holy name and dispense His pure and perfect justice. For a great many people, the day of the Lord will be terrifying. What a shock when they behold this Jesus whom they tried to shove back into a Sunday School room. Horror will strike their hearts as the scene in Revelation 19:11-16 unfolds. They'll cry:

> *I saw heaven standing open and there before me was a white horse, whose rider is called Faithful and True. With justice he judges and makes war. His eyes are like blazing fire, and on his head are many crowns. He has a name written on him that no one knows but he himself. He is dressed in a robe dipped in blood, and his name is the Word of God. The armies of heaven were following him, riding on white horses and dressed in fine linen, white and clean. Out of his mouth comes a sharp sword with which to strike down the nations. "He will rule them with an iron scepter." He treads the winepress of the fury of the wrath of God Almighty. On his robe and on his thigh he has this name written: KING OF KINGS AND LORD OF LORDS.*

These symbols aren't clunky at all; they're frightening! As an artist, I could not paint it, nor would I want to. Eyes like blazing fire? A robe dipped in blood? This is no senile benevolent grandfather who drowsily wished human beings well while they were on earth, a God to be pitied or felt sorry for. This is the great and terrible Lord, the consuming fire Himself. "See, the Lord is coming with fire, and his chariots are like a whirlwind; he will bring down his anger with fury, and his rebuke with flames of fire. For with fire and with his sword the Lord will execute judgment upon all men, and many will be those slain by the Lord" (Isaiah 66:15-16).

 Name at least four acquaintances who, as far as you know, are not prepared to meet the judgment of God. Write their names in the margin.

What are you presently doing to reach them for Christ and heaven?

❑ praying for them daily
❑ seeking to build witnessing relationships
❑ praying for others who may be able to reach them
❑ looking for practical ways to minister to them
❑ actively sharing the gospel with them
❑ other _____

The pictures in Isaiah 66 and Revelation 19 are not a pretty sight for "it is a dreadful thing to fall into the hands of the living God" (Hebrews 10:31). The same mouth that spoke peace and reconciliation will one day emit the sharp sword of judgment. The same eyes that glowed with compassion will one day blaze with fire. Is this the Rose of Sharon, the Lily of the valleys, my Bridegroom? Yes, this same Jesus, into whose loving hands I first fell, is the dreadful living God.

Lover and Avenger? He is perfectly one and the same. He is altogether loving in His justice, and just in His love. Because He is perfect, His justice is pure.

How Will I Feel on That Terrible Day?

Once in heaven, we will know in every fiber of our being, beyond a shadow of a doubt that whatever the Judge declares about us is true. As He says we are, so are we. No more, no less. If the Judge rules we were righteous in Christ, then "Hallelujah!" If He declares us unrighteous, wicked, and steeped in selfishness, then "curse me! I knew it all along." The self-evident truth about you or me will be clear to everyone.

As uncanny as it seems to us now, we won't cringe or cower on the great and terrible day of the Lord. Oddly, we will rejoice. This sounds insane because our human sense of compassion abhors the idea of justice being executed with unbridled sound and fury. On earth, justice is served as prisoners are quietly escorted from death row to chambers where hushed groups of people sit behind soundproofed windows and, without emotion, watch death happen.

But not in heaven. There, judgment is full of emotion.

 In the margin read Revelation 15:2-3 and 18:20. Underline how the believers react to seeing the judgment of God fall on unbelievers.

I saw what looked like a sea of glass mixed with fire and, standing beside the sea, those who had been victorious over the beast and his image and over the number of his name. They held harps given them by God and sang the song of Moses the servant of God and the song of the Lamb: "Great and marvelous are your deeds, Lord God Almighty. Just and true are your ways, King of the ages."
—Revelation 15:2-3

Rejoice over her, O heaven! Rejoice, saints and apostles and prophets! God has judged her for the way she treated you.
—Revelation 18:20

Does the rejoicing in these passages surprise you in any way? ❏ Yes ❏ No

Smack-dab in the middle of the apocalypse, as bowls of wrath are being poured out with smoke and fire, we are found singing and rejoicing while watching the judgment. The day of Christ will be a great and terrible day. Great for the righteous and terrible for the unrighteous. I'm just grateful that Scripture speaks of that time as only "a day." It may mean the great judgment will be swift. After all, "there are only two kinds of people in the end: those who say to God, 'Thy will be done,' and those to whom God says, in the end, 'Thy will be done.' All that are in Hell, choose it."[48]

For all the people who insisted "My will be done!" God will no longer strive with them, either by pointing to His glory in creation or by preaching to them from the gospel. For those who turn their backs on Christ, there is no heaven.

God's Perfect Timing

One day Jesus is going to return and finish Isaiah 61:2. He will judge the living and the dead, crush the wicked, and punish rebellious, impudent evildoers. He will upset nations and overthrow kings and rulers. He will institute the day of vengeance of our God.

This scene tempers my pleas for the soon return of Christ. I pray, "Come quickly, Lord Jesus," but I remember those who, unless they come to profess Christ as Savior, will end up getting trampled in the grapes of God's wrath.

Please hold off a bit longer that great and dreadful day of the Lord!

Still, I need to remember that God's timing is perfect. You and I have a job to do, just as the disciples were reminded when they asked Jesus when He would come back. The Lord said to them, "It is not for you to know the times or dates the Father has set by his own authority. But you will receive power ... and you will be my witnesses in Jerusalem, and in all Judea and Samaria, and to the ends of the earth" (Acts 1:8).

I need to be bothered enough to witness.

I need not bother myself with God's timing. I simply need to be bothered enough to witness. While Christ is in heaven, He is proclaiming through us the year of the Lord's favor. He is carrying out His agenda of compassion and forgiveness through you and me. He is still the tender, merciful Shepherd, looking for more people to rescue, searching for lost men and women on whom He can gladly bestow salvation.

So when I begin to lean on the windowsill of eternity and pine for my Savior to fulfill His promise to return, I bite my lip and recall 2 Peter 3:9: "The Lord is not slow in keeping his promise, as some understand slowness. He is patient with you, not wanting anyone to perish, but everyone to come to repentance." That's all the reminder I need to get away from that windowsill and go rescue the perishing.

 Write your own paraphrase of 2 Peter 3:9. Reword the verse to apply specifically to your friends and neighbors.

_____

_____

I can sum up 2 Peter 3:9 with this paraphrase: "The Lord is not slow in finishing His sentences, as some understand slowness. He is holding off the last part of Isaiah 61:2 so that, heaven willing, my neighbor, my relatives, and the people who work in my community will come to repentance."

Oh, how gracious of Jesus, how patient. How kind of our God, how merciful. Until the King of kings and Lord of lords returns with eyes of blazing fire, robe of blood, and sword and fury, you and I better get out there and proclaim the year of the Lord's favor.

Crown Him with Many Crowns

Is your blood pressure a notch higher like mine right now? Maybe you are feeling like me—awash in delight, yet reverent in fear, tingling with joy, yet trembling with holy respect. Our God is an awesome God.

I believe we are in the twilight of our hardships as well as the twilight of the world's history. I believe the days are short. My closing words for you are "Make the most of every opportunity" (Colossians 4:5). Oh, if we could only realize how short life is. James 4:14 says, "What is your life? You are a mist that appears for a little while and then vanishes." If we need another nudge, Isaiah 40:6-7 says, "All men are like grass ... the grass withers and the flowers fall, because the breath of the Lord blows on them. Surely the people are grass." Therefore make every effort. The days are evil. Redeem the time.

Make the most of your moments.

I'll see you at the wedding feast!

Make the most of your moments.

You have reached the end of this study, but only the beginning of what we will one day experience of heaven. Previously I have asked you to review units and summarize what you have learned. Now think back over this study. What insights have made the greatest impact on your understanding of heaven?

_____

_____

What three actions do you most need to take as a result of this study?

_____

_____

_____

Write a prayer expressing whatever emotions or commitments you bring away from your study of heaven.

_____

_____

_____

_____

Endnotes

1. This idea is from Harry Blamires *Knowing the Truth about Heaven and Hell,* (Ann Arbor, MI: Servant Books, 1988), 111.
2. This idea is from the writings of Nathaniel Hawthorne.
3. Robert Jastrow and Malcolm Thompson, *Astronomy; Fundamentals and Frontiers,* (Santa Barbara: John Wiley, 1977), 4, 12.
4. This idea is from A.W. Tozer's book *The Knowledge of the Holy.* (San Francisco: Harper Collins, 1992)
5. C. S. Lewis, *The Problem of Pain,* (New York: Macmillan: New York, Inc., 1962).
6. Will L. Thompson, "Softly and Tenderly."
7. Robert S. Sassone, *The Tiniest Humans,* (Stafford, VA: American Life League, 1995), viii.
8. This idea was suggested to me by my reading of C.H. Spurgeon.
9. Charles Tindley, "When the Morning Comes."
10. C. S. Lewis, *The Four Loves,* (New York: Harcourt, Brace, Jovanovich, 1960), 126.
11. C. S. Lewis, *George MacDonald: An Anthology* (New York: Macmillan, 1978), 8.
12. Dr. John H. Gerstner, *The Rational Biblical Theology of Jonathan Edwards,* (Orlando: Berea Publications, Ligonier Ministries, 1993), 552.
13. This idea was suggested to me in a personal letter from David Parrish.
14. A. E. Brumley, "This World Is Not My Home," (Glendale, CA: Praise Book Publications, 1951), 111. Used by permission.
15. Malcolm Muggeridge, *Jesus Rediscovered,* (New York: Doubleday, 1979), 47-48.
16. Peter Kreeft, *Heaven,* (San Fransisco: Ignatius Press, 1989), 66.
17. This idea was suggested to me in Peter Kreft's book, *Heaven.*
18. This idea is from Tim Stafford, *Knowing the Face of God,* (Grand Rapids: Zondervan, 1989), 182.
19. Kreeft, 121-122.
20. Sheldon Vanauken, *A Severe Mercy,* (San Fransisco: Harper & Row, 1977), 200, 202.
21. C. S. Lewis, *A Grief Observed,* (New York: Bantam Books, 1976), 16.
22. Joni Mitchell, "Woodstock." Copyright 1969 Siquomb Publishing Corp. Used by permission. All rights reserved.
23. Kreeft, 83.

24. Madame Jeanne Guyon, *Spiritual Torrents* (Auburn, ME: The Seed Sowers Christian Books Publishing House, 1980), 99.
25. Edythe Draper, *Draper's Book of Quotations for the Christian World* (Wheaton, IL: Tyndale House, 1992), 305.
26. Jerry Leiber and Mike Stoller, "Is That All There Is?" ©1966 Jerry Leiber and Mike Stoller Music. All rights reserved. Used by permission.
27. Kreeft, 44.
28. C. S. Lewis, *The Weight of Glory,* (Grand Rapids: Eerdmans, 1949), 12.
29. The ideas in these four paragraphs are derived from C. S. Lewis, *The Four Loves.*
30. Sharalee Lucas, "I See Jesus in You," (Nashville: Rambo-McGuire Music, 1986). Used by permission.
31. Lewis, *Weight of Glory,* 15.
32. Idea from Augustine, *Ennarationes in Pslamos* 127.9.
33. Augustine, *Confessions* I.I.
34. John MacAurthur, *Heaven* tape series, (Panorama City, CA: Grace to You, 1987).
35. Reginald Heber, "Holy, Holy, Holy."
36. Matthew Bridges, "Crown Him with Many Crowns."
37. Stafford, 221.
38. Samuel Rutherford, *Letters.*
39. Idea fom the writings of Bishop J. C. Ryle.
40. J. C. Ryle, *Holiness,* (Cambridge: James Clarke), 43-45.
41. Idea suggested by the writings of Andrew Greeley.
42. Idea from Kreeft, 124-161.
43. Kreeft, 96.
44. These ideas were borrowed from C. S. Lewis' *Till We Have Faces.*
45. William R. Featherton and Adoniram J. Gordon, "My Jesus, I Love Thee."
46. Ravi Zacharias, *The Veritas Forum at Harvard University Tape Series,* (Norcross, GA: Ravi Zacharias International Ministries, 1992).
47. This idea is from Dr. Jack Miller, Westminster Theological Seminary.
48. Lewis, *The Inspirational Writings of C. S. Lewis,* 382.

Group Leader Guide
By Dale W. McCleskey

Each week this leader guide will give you suggestions for processing what you and your group members have studied during the week. This resource should not be used to restrict group members' sharing during the sessions. Be flexible, prepared to pick up on members' interests. Adapt the suggested plan to fit your situation. Use the group time to encourage members to faithfully complete the unit assignments.

This study is designed to include the video available in *Heaven...Your Real Home Leader Kit,* along with your workbook. If you cannot obtain the video, you can still do this study effectively; however, I encourage you to use the video if at all possible. Joni's personal presence through the video will greatly enhance your study.

If you are using the video, play the appropriate segment to begin each session. As an incentive to be on time, stress that members will miss the video if they come late. Week 8 (Unit 7) has two video segments, one to be played at the beginning of the session and one to close out the study.

Some of the activities call for small group discussion. If your group has fewer than eight in attendance, simply do all the activities together. If you have eight or more members, divide into subgroups of threes (triads) for the first few suggested activities each week. Then allow members to report in the large group what they have learned in their triads. Encourage members to listen carefully to each other. Your group can be a powerful blessing as members learn and apply listening skills. When an activity calls for brainstorming or compiling a list, write responses on a tearsheet or chalkboard.

I have given you more suggested questions or activities than you can cover in a one-hour session. You will need to select the activities that best fit your group.

Introductory Session

Begin the study by asking each member to compose a sentence expressing his or her eagerness for life in heaven. Ask members to write the sentence on the inside front cover of their books. State, *Since the purpose of this study is to increase your passion for heaven, you will compare your attitude at the end of the study with the statement you have just written.*

Share your personal enthusiasm for the study. Explain that members will complete five daily lessons that make up a unit. Then

the group will gather weekly to talk about what they have learned, share insights, fellowship, and pray together. If you are using the video explain that Joni will be sharing a five-to-seven-minute personal overview with the group each week. Point out that the video contains material not included in the book.

Show the 20-minute introductory video message. Lead members in discussing what aspect of the video most interests or excites them.

Give members opportunity to glance through the book. Ask them to make a note of any questions they wish to discuss as they read and to bring their questions to group time. Be certain you allow time for questions or comments as a part of each session's activities.

Call attention to several of the learning activities. Encourage members to be diligent in completing their study assignments. As you go through the study, refer often to the actual work members have done in their books. In this way you can both encourage them to do their homework and hold them accountable. After the first week or two members will know that completing their work is important.

As time permits, ask several probing questions about heaven to stimulate interest, such as what will we look like? what will we do? Don't attempt to deal with the questions; simply allow comments.

Remind members that they need to complete the introduction and unit 1 before the next meeting.

Close with prayer for God's guidance throughout the study.

Unit 1
What's So Great About Heaven?

Show the video (optional).

1. Ask, *Why do many descriptions of heaven detract from our wanting to go there?* Follow that discussion with: *Have you sometimes felt that the loss of certain things would make heaven less than desirable? If so, explain.*

2. State, *Much of what we have thought about heaven comes from culture rather than Scripture. (For example, many people believe that those who die become angels.) To what degree do you think people generally believe what they have heard as opposed to carefully searching the Scriptures?* Encourage members to covenant with you to base their views on Scripture rather than tradition/hearsay.

3. Review the story of Steve and the Chicago road sign (p. 14). Ask group members to share possible ways they may have hit their heads on a road sign, such as, stopped at a confusing symbol without asking what greater reality the symbol represents.

4. Divide the group into triads. Instruct triads to discuss the life review learning activity from page 17. Ask groups to compile a list of

things that were once important to them but have lost importance. Then reconvene the large group and call for reports. Invite response to how the lists relate to their attitudes about heaven.

5. Invite members to share their answers to the activity on page 19, when they felt, "get me outta here!"

6. Ask members how they prioritized the list of benefits of heaven (p. 20). Ask, *Why do you suppose various people value the benefits in different ways?*

7. Suggest that lesson 4 was the most intellectually challenging section in the unit. Ask, *What insight did you gain from the lesson? What question(s) did you have?*

8. Ask volunteers to share Scriptures or concepts they have identified that increase their eagerness and passion for heaven.

Pray for each member that through this study they will develop a passion for God and for heaven.

Unit 2
Who Are We in Heaven?

Show video (optional).

Divide the group into triads. Consider creative methods to rotate the members of the triads so that all members will have a greater chance to get to know each other. For example, tape pictures of animals under chairs and put together "animal triads." Give the following instructions one at a time as triads complete each previous exercise:

1. Share the one thing you most look forward to or have apprehensions about regarding your new, resurrected body.

2. Describe your experience with the field trip (p. 33).

3. Discuss the "heart-check" statements on page 34.

4. Share personal examples of the battle described in Romans 7:24-25 (p. 34).

5. Compile a list of ways to resist temptation from page 36.

6. Share some of the names on your "top 10" list, (p. 41) and explain your choices.

7. Tell about a friend who has stuck with you through the years.

As a final item in triad time, allow each member opportunity either to give or withhold permission for triad members to repeat their stories to the large group.

In the large group:

1. Ask the group, *Did the statement in Deuteronomy 8:2-3, that God causes your "hungries," surprise you? Why or why not?*

2. If you know the tune, sing together: "We Will Understand It Better By and By" (p. 39).

3. Brainstorm characteristics of God you have come to appreciate through seeing them lived out by friends. Allow an opportunity for group members to affirm each other.

4. Call for a triad report: What did some of the members look forward to about their new bodies? Who were some people on the "top ten" lists? Use these reports as a time to increase fellowship and laugh together. Ask if anyone heard a particularly touching story of a "through the years" friend. Remind the group that they can only share a story with permission.

5. Ask, *In what way has your study this week changed: 1) your thinking about heaven, 2) your passion for heaven.*

Close with prayer by calling on one or more group members to voice a prayer of thanksgiving for our heavenly home.

Unit 3
What Will We Do in Heaven?

Show video (optional).
Give triads the following assignments one at a time. Remind triad members to listen closely so as to report with permission.

1. Answer, *How do you tend to think God feels about you?* (p. 51)

2. Discuss who you would like to see the Lord honor (p. 53).

3. Discuss how your study of the judgment has affected your attitudes about redemption and judgment (pp.57-58).

In the large group:

1. Brainstorm reasons why we will not be envious in heaven (p. 54).

2. Call for members to post the pictures they drew this week (p. 62). Ask volunteers to share the story behind their pictures.

3. Call for reports from triads concerning who they desired to see honored.

4. Ask, *What job would you like to do in heaven?* (p. 66) *What thought most encourages you about service in heaven?*

5. Ask, *How do you feel about the prospect of judging angels? demons? Does ultimate justice for a persecution bring comfort?*

Close with sentence prayers of gratitude for all of heaven's promises.

Unit 4
Why Don't We Fit on Earth?

Show video (optional).
In triads do the following activities/answer questions:

1. Share your paraphrase of Psalm 137:5. Pray for each other as you seek to develop a deeper loyalty to Christ.

2. Describe a "wheelchair" in your life: a hurt, heartbreak, or disability that prompts you to look to heaven.

3. Answer the question, *According to Malcolm Muggeridge, why is feeling at home here on earth a disaster?*

4. Develop a list of reasons why heaven is a better country (p. 76). Choose the top five reasons and prioritize the list.

5. Share an experience of homesickness. Describe how homesickness feels.

In the large group:

1. Have members turn to the rating exercise on page 80. On a chalkboard or large piece of paper, draw a vertical line with the words "smears and smudges" at one end and "fine linen" at the other. Ask everyone to come to the board and place a dot on the line to indicate how they see themselves. Ask everyone to do this together using the "pandemonium method"—all members come up at the same time and mark on the board as quickly as they can.

Then ask those members who wish to do so to share why they marked the spot they chose. Ask if the study this week affected how they see themselves.

2. Respond to the debate-team assignment (p. 82). Lead the group to list as many arguments as possible.

3. Ask someone to share a particularly touching account of homesickness she heard in the triad, with the original storyteller's permission, of course.

4. Receive reports from triads on why heaven is a "better country."

5. Brainstorm ways you can introduce constructive heavenly-mindedness into your world this week.

Close with prayer thanking God for instilling in us the longing for a home other than earth.

Unit 5
Why Do We Fit in Heaven?

Show video (optional).

In triads do the following activities/answer questions:

1. Share your responses to the activity at the top of page 94—a gift you wanted but that did not satisfy. Then share responses to the activity at the bottom of the same page.

2. Describe the most ecstatic experience in your life (p. 97). Listen closely to your triad partners because you may be asked to tell one of their stories.

3. Compile a list of treasures you will receive in completed form in heaven (p. 103). Prepare a report for the large group.

In the large group:

1. Ask, *Have you ever known someone who expected a romantic relationship to do the impossible—to keep him/her in a state of continual ecstacy* (p. 98)? Discuss the limits of earthly relationships.

2. Discuss how love for another person can become idolatry (p. 99).

3. Ask, *How does a relationship with Jesus affect your use of time, interests, and priorities?* (p.102)

4. Ask, *What practical differences do you suppose living in the present tense regarding heaven will make in your life (p. 105)?*

5. Ask members to share, with permission, any description of a particularly ecstatic experience they heard in their triads. Then ask what these feelings of temporary ecstasy say about heaven.

6. Compare lists of treasures (activity 3 in triads). Lead the group to select from the lists the top five treasures.

7. Ask members to share something they have discovered about heaven this week or something that has changed their passion for heaven. Conclude with prayer time together.

Unit 6
How Does Heaven Help Me Handle Today?

Show video (optional).
In triads do the following activities/answer questions:

1. Share three things that trouble you now but will not pass the "end of time" test (p. 114).

2. Share examples of a painful experience that seemed like an eternity at the time but that now seems like a blip on the screen of life (p. 115).

3. Work together to draft an explanation to a hostile world about the connection between heaven and suffering (p. 117). Prepare to share statements with the large group.

4. Compare paraphrases of Psalm 73:25-26.

In the large group:

1. Receive reports from the triads of their answers to assignment #3 above. Discuss the connection between suffering and heaven.

2. Brainstorm a checklist of character traits we want to clean from our hearts (p. 122).

3. Discuss the two learning activities on page 128. Ask, *How does Jesus' resurrection affect your attitude about suffering? death? the death of your loved ones?*

4. Ask, *How has this week's study affected your feelings about suffering?* Be sensitive to persons in the group who may be dealing with a recent loss or ongoing health or relational concern. Do not try

to talk them out of their feelings. As Joni readily admits, she went through a time of anger and resentment initially.

5. Close the session in silent prayer. Lead the group to pray through the list of character traits on page 122.

Unit 7
How Do I Get Ready for Heaven?

Show video (optional). Save "Joni's Farewell" until end of session.
In triads do the following activities/answer questions:

1. Compare one-sentence summaries of the parable of the 10 virgins (p. 133).

2. Discuss what it does and does not mean to "wait on the Lord." Compile two lists to share with the large group.

3. Share the time and place when you decided to set your hearts and minds on heavenly glories (p. 134). Describe what difference that commitment makes in your daily decisions.

4. Discuss the roles Jesus plays in our lives (p. 135) and share which roles are most important in your life.

5. Share experiences from a "walk with God" exercise (p. 137).

6. Relate a personal experience when God used "divine judo" for your good (p. 145).

In the large group:

1. Brainstorm songs you look forward to singing in heaven (p. 142). If the group is willing, sing a verse of some of the songs.

2. Call for reports from the triads' discussions of "divine judo" (p. 145).

3. Ask, *How does the assurance in Hebrews 2:10 that Jesus became perfect through suffering affect your attitude about your own thorns, burdens, and crosses?*

4. Ask, *How has this study affected your attitude about heaven? your love for the Lord?*

5. Ask, *What has made the greatest impact on your understanding of Scripture and of heaven?*

6. Lead members to look at what they wrote on the inside front cover of their books in the Introductory Session (first activity). Ask if anyone would want to change or add to his statement. Allow time for responses.

Show the video "Joni's Farewell" (optional).

Close the study with a time of group prayer. Ask each member to pray for the person on his or her left. Your group may want to plan some follow-up study or fellowship together.

HEAVEN
Gift Boutique

Give your customers a reminder of their heart's true home with these selections from the *Heaven* Gift Boutique. Joni Eareckson Tada's evocative artwork from her new book, *Heaven,* comes in gorgeous full color in this attractive assortment. From a Daybreak® perpetual calendar that will add a splash of color and inspiration to every day, to notecards and stationery that let friends and family remember heaven as they remember each other, there's something here for everyone. Joni's incredible imagery is sure to please both the eye and heart, in formats that meet a variety of needs.

Available at Baptist Bookstores
and Lifeway Christian Stores
or by calling

1-800-233-1123

HEAVEN DAYBREAK®
ISBN 0-310-96555-1
5x4, 368 Pages Perpetual Calendar
Retail Price
$9.99

HEAVEN NOTECARDS
ISBN 0-310-96553-5
10 full-color notecards and 10 envelopes
Retail Price
$4.99

HEAVEN STATIONERY
ISBN 0-310-96552-7
Includes 16 full-color stationery sheets
and 10 envelopes
Retail Price
$8.99

HEAVEN JOURNAL
ISBN 0-310-96554-3
A beautiful way to chronicle your walk with God!
With full-color cover and one-color interior pages.
Retail Price
$7.99

ZondervanPublishingHouse

LEARN ABOUT HEAVEN and life on earth will never be the same.

Heaven

Heaven...Your Real Home

by Joni Eareckson Tada

- Does heaven help me handle today?
- How can I get ready for heaven?

In her own heartwarming, personal style Joni shares the incredible hope of heaven and how what we do here on earth has a direct bearing on how we will live there. This intriguing study helps you set your heart on things above, where your true treasure lies. Join us for this eight-week study about heaven, our eternal home.

MAYBE, like most people, you're caught up in the here and now and find it difficult to grasp how real heaven is. In this small-group study, *Heaven...Your Real Home*, you'll find answers to these thought-provoking questions:

- What will heaven be like?
- Why don't we fit on earth?
- Why do we fit in heaven?

Heaven ...Your Real Home

Heaven ...Your Real Home

Heaven ...A Place to Belong
Collegiate Edition

Heaven ...Your Real Home
Youth Edition

Heaven...Your Real Home, Adult Edition
7201-10 $9.95

Heaven...Your Real Home Leader Kit
Video-driven kit contains Joni's personal testimony, brief vignettes that capture the heart of each week's session, and a brief promotional segment. Kit also includes one copy of adult member book.
7700-78 $59.95

Prices subject to change without notice.

Heaven...A Place to Belong, Collegiate Edition
Six-session interactive member book includes teaching suggestions at the end of the book.
7201-18 $9.95

Heaven...Your Real Home, Youth Edition
Eight-session interactive workbook with facilitator's suggestions at the end of the book.
7201-06 $9.95

Write, call, or fax Customer Service Center, 127 Ninth Avenue, North; Nashville, TN 37234; **1-800-458 2772. Fax: (615) 251-5933.**